How to Become Smarter

Discover How to Increase Intelligence and Boost Brainpower

by Cameron Jessup

Table of Contents

Introduction

Just as your muscles can be trained to help you become stronger, the many functions of your brain, which make up your overall intelligence, can also be trained to help you become smarter. It is the belief of modern psychology that the repetition of certain exercises can produce more fluid and agile thinking, better problem-solving capability, and a stronger short term memory.

With regard to long term memory and long term learning in general, we've known for a long time that the more you read, experience, and study, the more you will produce positive contributions to your level of, what psychologists call, "crystallized" intelligence. Crystallized intelligence is life learning, the culmination of everything you've experienced and retained as a human. Its corollary, known as "fluid intelligence," is your ability to manipulate figures and facts in your head, to analyze, and be creative.

There are ways for you to dramatically improve both your crystallized and fluid intelligence. For example, it's been proven that working puzzles, such as Sudoku, exercises your brain and contributes positively to your fluid intelligence. Reading a book on a famous historical figure, in turn, will contribute to your overall crystallized intelligence. Reading a book on the complex philosophies of Arthur Schopenhauer will probably increase both your crystallized and fluid intelligence levels simultaneously. In the following chapters, we'll discuss a multitude of techniques, exercises, as well as dietary, pharmaceutical, and lifestyle choices, that will increase your intelligence and boost your brain power!

Chapter 1: The Intelligent Lifestyle

If you're serious about becoming smarter, you need to build a firm foundation for intellectual development. You can make perhaps the biggest impact by adopting an "intelligent lifestyle." Think about your routines, what you spend your time doing and with whom you associate. Are you more inclined to watch brainless television after you get home from work, or do you crack open a book? Do you visit local museums and exhibits on the weekends, or do you down a six pack of beer and consume mindless television? You certainly don't need to (and you really shouldn't) rid your life of everything fun in your quest for better brain power, but you *must* be aware of how the lifestyle choices you make affect you.

Don't worry, adopting an intelligent lifestyle doesn't have to be daunting. Begin with small and simple changes, like spicing your life up by boldly exploring and learning about new things. Here are a few small and simple habits you can adopt that will add novel elements to your life and ultimately increase your general intelligence.

Adventures in Grocery Shopping:

From this point forward, whenever you go grocery shopping, purchase one food item that you know little to nothing about. You can often find exotic fruits or vegetables that you've never encountered, perhaps a Vietnamese dragon fruit, a parsnip, a star fruit, or an Asian pear. If you have no idea how to go about preparing your novelty item, then you know you've made a good selection. Use the internet to find written or video instructions on how to prepare your item and who knows, maybe you'll not only learn about a new food, but find something you'll enjoy eating for years to come. Every new element of novelty you introduce into your life adds to your crystallized intelligence, and, to some extent, exercises your fluid intelligence by forcing you to use your brain to learn and experience something new.

Take a New Route Home from Work:

It's shocking how much unexplored territory you can discover just around the corner in your own hometown. We tend to lock ourselves into patterns when travelling from one place to another locally, often finding ourselves too busy to simply get in our cars and explore for the sake of exploring. We've lost sight of the fact that automobiles are extraordinary instruments, a privilege of modernity, that allow us to explore vast expanses of territory in a relatively short amount of time. Try and identify a few different routes you can take while driving to and from work, even if they're longer than your standard routes. Exposing yourself to new sensory input prevents your mind (and spirit) from growing dull and stimulates new ideas.

Make a New Friend:

It's easy to always interact with the same people. Try striking up a conversation at a coffee shop, bar, or community event. Everyone, in their own way, has something unique to teach you or share with you. Avoid pigeonholing people to fit preconceived stereotypes. We do this instinctually to feel comfortable and in-control during our interactions with new people. Instead of being fearful, try being receptive and optimistic about what you might learn from a stranger.

Now, if you're really serious about self-improvement, and are able to be highly flexible when making lifestyle choices, then you can consider some more dramatic changes, such as:

Change Your Job:

If your work-a-day life has gotten stale, then why not seek out something new that will broaden your overall life experience. Maybe you don't even need to leave your company, just transfer to a different position. Some jobs in government, the military, and in larger corporations rotate people around frequently in order to keep them fresh and intellectually stimulated. If you're in a smaller company or have a highly specialized skill, then it may not be so easy to pull out and change jobs on a dime. A less drastic option would be to take on a part time job that will provide a new and different environment. Or maybe, it's time to work on getting a new skill.

Go Back to School:

Could there be any simpler path to gaining smarts then getting back in the classroom? Reconnecting with academia will put you in touch with new people and new ideas. You'll read, you'll study, you'll solve problems and you will become more intelligent. If getting another degree is something you cannot commit time to, enroll in a short course for a particular skill, like learning a foreign language or basic accounting and finance management. There are even online classes where you can learn how to bake or cook in your own kitchen or learn a computer programming language on your own time.

Live in a Foreign Country:

Not only will living in a foreign country likely present you with an opportunity to learn a new language, but you'll also be exposed to a myriad of novelty. New culture, new customs, new food, new ways of life, your brain won't have any choice but to adapt and expand as it helps you process your new environment. If you are enrolled in school as well, you can kill two birds by studying abroad.

Another lifestyle choice that will strengthen your foundation for intellectual growth is your pursuit of physical, dietary, and emotional well-being. If you're getting regular exercise and you're in good cardiovascular health, then your brain is benefitting as well as every other organ in your body. Aim for a lifestyle that promotes comprehensive wellness and you'll find that your intellectual health will follow in tow.

Speaking of being healthy, if you want to improve your intelligence, take some time away from technology. The next time you go on a road trip, put the GPS navigator in the trunk and fold out an old-school road map. You may find this not only more intellectually stimulating, but fun as well. Maps let you take in an expansive panorama of a region, its roadways, landmarks, and topography, whereas your GPS system just tells you where to turn. How boring.

Another area where technology interferes with good mental hygiene is arithmetic. Practice manipulating numbers using the calculator between your ears. Even if you're a person who "sucks at math," try to do it anyways. You'll get more proficient and more confident over time, and you'll be refining your fluid intelligence.

An intelligent lifestyle is the baseline for becoming a smarter person, but of course, most people can't follow every lifestyle choice recommended here. Nor is this an exhaustive list of lifestyle adjustments that you can make to improve your intelligence. You should continually be on the look-out for original ways to alter your routines and challenge your comfort levels. Choose a new intellectually healthy habit every month and stick with it. Little by little you'll transform yourself into an intellectual powerhouse.

Chapter 2: Building an Intelligent Skill Set

Reading, writing, chess, puzzles—these are activities that require certain skills. Developing these skills can contribute to your overall fluid and crystallized intelligence. Here are a few skills you can pursue that will help you thrive intellectually:

Meditation:

The fundamental mind, body, spirit connection can be strengthened through the practice of meditation. Meditation helps your attention span, which in turn will improve your working memory, which is the foundation of fluid intelligence. Meditation can also improve your general emotional and physical health, and both of these factors contribute to your intellectual prowess.

Meditation is a skill that can be taught easily, but is best learned slowly. Start by researching and choosing a technique. Find instruction, either at a local Sanga or on the internet. Begin with short sits; five or ten minutes daily is a good way to begin your practice.

Art:

When you face the challenge of reflecting the world around you by crafting artwork, you force yourself into observing and thinking about small details you'd ordinarily overlook. There's no way to develop an artistic skill without expanding and challenging your habitual way of thinking and learning. This is why the creation of art can be a powerful intellectual stimulant. Whatever medium you choose to work with—painting, drawing, sculpture—art will allow you to connect the forms of observable reality with the enhancements of the imagination. This is what your brain was made for. To help you get started, you can get a book on the medium you wish to pursue, and/or, you can investigate local art classes at your community center or elsewhere. These classes are often affordable and taught by an experienced artist.

Writing:

The skill of writing hybridizes puzzle solving with limitless imagination. There is no guarantee that an idea you wish to express, or a scene you wish to illustrate, is easily translatable into words. To achieve competence in writing, you must read a lot and write a lot. You must learn to do more with less, understanding how people absorb information from the written word, understanding which words flow and which words distract, and forging a connection with the reader that will prove communicative and valuable. The act of learning to balance all of these variables effectively will undoubtedly contribute to your fluid intelligence.

Reading:

Reading is to your crystallized intelligence what writing is to your fluid intelligence. Reading books brings you into new arenas of knowledge, guided by an intellectual presence (the narrator or author) who is completely foreign to you. He or she may be from a totally different part of the world or even from a totally different time, offering you an internal and psychologically intimate perspective on life that you just won't be able to find on a television or movie screen.

Not to say that reading can't also augment your fluid intelligence as well. Reading at a good pace and exerting focus to comprehend supports the development of cognitive skill and is a wonderful workout for your brain.

Learning a New Language:

If you've ever studied a new language before, then you're probably aware of how language study can spawn unique insights into human psychology and cognition. Learning how a whole other people has come to symbolize and consider the universe will inevitably lead to veritable torrents of inbound intellectual stimulation.

Ideally you'd learn a new language in a foreign country, but if you're homebound, you can still take a class or buy a book or DVDs. Some communities even facilitate cultural exchanges where you can trade language proficiencies with someone seeking to learn English.

Learn a Sport:

Seeing as how the body-mind connection is inextricable, taking up a new physical hobby is a great way to boost both your physical and mental acumens. Studies show that children who are active do better academically and have a higher chance of pursuing post-graduate education. Many sports require both physical and mental toughness. Tennis and golf, for instance, are known for their emphasis on persistent mental focus. Even if you're simply at the gym lifting weights or running, you're still giving yourself an ideal opportunity to practice mental discipline. Furthermore, a lot of runners and weight-lifters are known to consume copious amounts of intellectually stimulating audio books or podcasts during their fitness routines.

Become a Gear Head:

Knowing your way around the inside of a car is like being a surgeon without so much pressure. Though there's a great deal of technical know-how that every gearhead has to learn on their own, there's also an element of artistry and intuition in play as well. Diagnosing and responding to car problems, or even just accomplishing routine maintenance, gives you a chance to confront and decipher a complex system with many moving parts. What more could your brain want?

Though this is clearly not an exhaustive list of possible mind-refining skills, hopefully this listing will provide you with an idea of what to consider when selecting a skill to learn. Maybe your job already requires you to exercise a great deal of fluid intelligence, and you'd be more inclined to take up reading or some other activity that would contribute to your crystallized intelligence. Maybe your job is monotonous and intellectually vapid, and you'd prefer to use your free time to engage in complex creative activity like art or writing. Figure out what skill pursuits make sense for you and best complement your lifestyle.

Chapter 3: Best of the Brain Foods

As with a healthy body, a healthy brain requires both exercise *and* diet to perform a peak levels. Here are some critical foodstuffs that will help keep you smart:

Anything with Omega 3s:

The neuron membranes (or walls) of our brains are made of benign fatty tissues. It's important for this tissue to be supported in order to ensure optimal communications between neurons. Omega 3 fatty acids, found in fish and fish oil, provide your brain with healthy infrastructure. You can get your fill of Omega 3 fatty acids by regularly eating fish or by taking Omega 3 supplements.

If you are worried about the mercury content in fish or fish byproducts, then you can add Chlorella to your Omega 3 intake. Chlorella is a marine-based superfood that, similar to its land-based cousin, Spirulina, is known for its detoxifying properties.

If you're inclined towards whole foods rather than supplements, wild salmon is a delicious, effective way to get yourself a good dose of Omega 3's.

Raw Cacao Hot Chocolate:

In Aztec dialect, "cacao" means "food of the gods." There are a whole host of reasons to love raw cacao. Among them, cacao is *the* richest food in antioxidants, carrying twice as many antioxidants per gram than acai berries. There is no other food with a higher concentration of magnesium, which relaxes muscles. And it also makes you smarter!

Raw cacao contains neuro-enhancers such as PEA (phenylethylamine), which can ward off depression and enhance one's attention capacity. It also contains anandamide, which is colloquially known as "the bliss chemical," and serotonin, which also improves our sense of wellbeing. The combination of this brain-healthy entourage of chemicals can help you fend off anxieties which distract and detract from your intellectual pursuits, while allowing you to focus comfortably and perform optimally in the face of intellectual challenges.

Matcha Green Tea:

First used over 800 years ago by monks in Japan, Matcha was noted to cause increases in alertness and concentration. Made from crushed and pulverized Gyokuro green tea leaves, Matcha Green Tea is bursting with phytonutrients and flavonoids.

Blueberries:

Animal studies have shown blueberries to be effective in combating the onset of age-related neural disorders such as Alzheimer's and dementia. Rat studies have shown that blueberries can improve learning capacity and motor skills. The main brain-boosting components of blueberries are flavonoids, which have been shown to improve reasoning skills, learning, decision making, verbal comprehension, and general cognitive functioning.

Pomegranate Juice:

David Perlmutter, MD, author of The Better Brain Book, posits that "Probably no part of the body is more sensitive to the damage from free radicals as the brain." This is why a diet rich in anti-oxidants is so important for those seeking optimized brain power. Pomegranate juice has an astoundingly high anti-oxidant count and is a great dietary choice for protecting the brain from harm.

Beans:

The brain, like the rest of the body, is dependent on glucose for fuel. But unlike other parts of the body, the brain doesn't have a storing mechanism in place for glucose and needs a constant influx of new supply. Eating a half cup of beans per day ensures your brain doesn't get gassed out due to air pockets in the glucose supply chain.

Nuts and Seeds:

Pumpkin seeds, flax seeds, walnuts, hazelnuts, Brazil nuts, filberts, almonds, cashews, all of them rich in vitamin E, these nuts and seeds can interrupt the tide of cognitive decline. A half a cup a day of good nuts should do the trick.

Avocadoes:

Avocadoes are rich in mono-saturate fat (good fat) which contributes to healthy blood flow to the brain and elsewhere. Avocadoes also lower blood pressure, high blood pressure being a significant contributor to cognitive decline.

Whole Grains and Wheat Germ:

Anything that improves circulation and heart health will inevitably contribute to a healthier brain. The brain is a vibrant organ that thrives on the abundance of nutrients procured through healthy blood flow. Whole grains such as brown rice, oatmeal, and whole grain bread, improve cardiovascular health. Wheat germ in particular are recognized as a superfood for the brain because it also contains Omega 3s and Vitamin E. If you're looking for a way to integrate wheat germ into your diet, try mixing it in your oatmeal or cold cereal.

Tomatoes:

Rich in lycopene, tomatoes can help build up your defenses against the free radicals that contribute to the onset of dementia and Alzheimer's.

Chapter 4: Intelligence Sharpening Games and Drills

A *New England Journal of Medicine* study found that adults who regularly participate in mentally stimulating activity are 63% less likely to develop dementia. Other studies have shown that brain functioning can be dramatically improved through games and drills (mental exercises) that force you to exert your brain power. Here are some examples of games you can play that will make you smarter!

Six Word Stories:

Take six words and write a coherent short story. It doesn't have to be good, but it should at least be clear, even if it's ridiculous. You will find this task to be a puzzle in and of itself, challenging in both an artistic and technical sense. Earnest Hemingway currently holds the informal record for the most compelling six word short story with: For sale, baby shoes, never worn.

Non-Dominant Day:

Try using your non-dominant hand as your dominant hand for a day. Put your mouse on the opposite side of your keyboard. Use your left (or right) hand to hold your eating utensils. Your brain will be forced to generate new neural pathways to accommodate these strange and unfamiliar movements. By the end of the day, you should notice that your switch-handed activities have grown somewhat easier thanks to your brain's adaptability.

Photo Analysis:

Find a photo depicting a busy and unfamiliar scene, maybe a picture of a crowded park with people, animals, games being played, dogs running around etc. Look at the photo for a minute and then put it away. Take out a sheet of paper and write down as many details about the photo as you can remember. Mark the photo with the day of the week and then do a different photo and mark it the next day. After you have a photo for every day of the week (you can just do 5 or 6 days weekly, if you want), repeat the exercise the following week. See how much better you do after a week's time. For the third week try looking at the photo for only 30 seconds rather than a minute but continue to exert your best focal energies on each photo. Do you do better or worse with the 30 second window? Keep track of your score (awarding yourself one point for each detail you recall) and repeat the experiment with a whole new set of photos, similar in their quantity of distinguishable details. If you find yourself becoming more proficient at this game over time, then it's safe bet that you're getting smarter!

The Colored Text Drill:

Do a google search for "Words written in the wrong colors." You'll find several pictures of text where the name of a color is spelled out using text in some other color. For example you might see the word brown spelled in black text. Take this listing and peruse through it naming each of the *colors you see* ignoring the words themselves. See how fast and accurate you are and whether your results improve through practice.

Numerical Pattern Gymnastics:

Take a high number, 3 or 4 digits long and count backwards by 5, 6, or 13. For example, start with 1300 and count backwards by 13: 1287, 1274, 1261… Do this all the way down to 0. This drill will train your mind to process numbers arithmetically.

Conscious Note Taking:

Too many people take notes just to have something to do with their hands. In the process they waste paper and look foolish. Taking notes properly will not only help you stay organized but can be an enriching mental exercise. In order to take notes well you have to be simultaneously listening to what's being said, thinking about what you need to know, and identifying what elements, once written down, will allow you to most easily work your way back through the most important pieces of the information presented. Use shorthand and abbreviations. Don't write down stuff that you already know and are not going to forget. Don't try and write down everything that's being said verbatim. And don't start making a note unless you are sure you're going to be able to transcribe your complete thought. Conscious note taking, when done well, is an incredibly involved and stimulating mental exercise.

Sudoku:

The popular Japanese number puzzle, Sudoku, is a fantastic exercise for your working memory, logical and spatial reasoning.

Online Games:

There are websites such as *Luminosity* that have games, which you can play online, designed to make you smarter. Many of these are memory games, logic games, sequencing games, or electronically rendered versions of the games discussed elsewhere in this chapter.

Chapter 5: Supplements to Assist

Do you have a clear weakness intellectually? Are you unable to focus? Is your memory rough around the edges? Do you struggle with staying alert and interested in the subject matter at hand? At the risk of sounding like a television ad for prescription drugs, you may be able to dramatically improve your cognitive functioning by using a prescription-grade or over-the-counter supplement to bolster your brain.

Ginko Biloba:

Ginko Biloba refers to the medicinal leaves found on the tree of the same name. For thousands of years Chinese medicine has made use of this tree, and in modern alternative medicine, Ginko Biloba is rumored to boost cognitive functioning, particularly memory. Ginko Biloba improves blood flow and is rich in anti-oxidants, but it's hard to say whether this supplement is worthy of its hype. Some studies have shown Ginko Biloba to produce a modest uptick in memory and cognitive speed while others could not identify a clear connection.

Vitamin D:

There are receptors for vitamin D in the central nervous system, specifically in the brain's hippocampus which regulates memory and spatial recognition. In this area of the body Vitamin D can regulate enzymes in the brain and the cerebrospinal fluid which contribute to neurotransmitter synthesis and nerve growth. Studies have shown that vitamin D deficiencies are associated with poorer performance on mental skills tests.

Vitamin D's relevance to neurological health is so significant that people who live in parts of the world with shorter daytimes or limited sunlight should introduce supplements into their diets to ensure they're getting enough vitamin D. Cod liver oil, beef, butter, and milk are good sources. Remember though, especially if you don't eat meat, not to take boat loads of vitamin D in pill form, as it is toxic in high quantities. Instead, pair your supplemental intake of Vitamin D with Vitamins A and K.

Theanine:

Imagine if you could have the alertness of coffee without the jitters. Theanine, found in green tea, provides a focused, calm feeling. Theanine can also be combined with caffeine for excellent Nootropic benefits.

Modafinil:

Modafinil is used to treat narcolepsy and sleep apnea, but is best known for its incredible Nootropic boost. Modafinil can keep you awake and fully engaged with whatever you're trying to focus on. It is a prescription drug, however, with some side effects and abuse potential.

Stimulants:

Dextroamphetamine (Adderall) and Methylphenidate (Ritalin) are neuro-stimulants that affect the brain's dopamine and norepinephrine functioning. Stimulants are commonly used as study drugs, as they allow the user to stay alert and focused for extraordinarily long lengths of time.

Stimulants have several significant side-effects such as weight loss, anxiety, and irritable bowel syndrome. There is also a very high potential for addiction and abuse with these drugs.

Melatonin:

Quality sleep is part and parcel to optimum intellectual functioning. Melatonin is a supplement that the body produces naturally when it needs to sleep, but often the body's natural supply isn't enough to cope with the forces of modernity. Our constant exposure to LCD screens and other lights can fool the body and prevent adequate melatonin production. Using melatonin supplements causes no discernable negative side effects and can dramatically improve your sleep quality.

Conclusion

Boosting your mental prowess is a very hot topic these days. One of the reasons for this is recent research showing that there really is a lot of wiggle room when it comes to intelligence dynamics, more so than previously thought. More research still needs to be done on the subject, but there's definitely a lot promise for those who are willing to work hard and make changes in order to become more intelligent.

Anyone of the games, drills, dietary or supplement choices, or lifestyle choices you choose to explore will enhance your intelligence in some way shape or form. Do some research, reflection and experimentation to find which methods will fit your goals, lifestyle, and body chemistry and follow through with your plan. When you commit to becoming a smarter, more optimized human being, your life, and contributions to society, can only change for the better. Good luck!

Finally, I'd like to thank you for purchasing this book! If you enjoyed it or found it helpful, I'd greatly appreciate it if you'd take a moment to leave a review on Amazon. Thank you!

Printed in Great Britain
by Amazon

Into Love

A Journey of Near-Death and Surrendering Into Love

TAMMY LEE ANDERSON

 SpiritLed
PRESS

Into Love Copyright © 2025 by Tammy Lee Anderson
Book One of the **INTO** Series
All rights reserved.
Published in the United States of America by SpiritLed Press

Foreword: Suzanne Giesemann
Cover Design: Kristina Konstantinova
Interior Design: Tammy Lee Anderson
Interior Spirit Art by Jon (*through:* Tammy Lee Anderson)

Cataloging-in-Publication Data now on file at Library of Congress

Tradepaper ISBN: 979-8-9986559-0-6
E-book ISBN: 979-8-9986559-1-3
Audio Book ISBN: 979-9986559-2-0
1st edition, Aug 2025

SpiritLed Press
Clovis, California USA
SpiritLedPress.com

To Rev. Bill McDonald
Without your unwavering encouragement,
this book might never have been completed.
Thank you from the depths of my heart.

To my sister, Terrie Pierce
My dearest and best friend—
A true earth angel.
I love you beyond words.

To all my Loved Ones in Spirit
You continue to inspire me
to live the best version of myself,
here, now, and always.

CONTENTS

ACKNOWLEDGMENTS

This book is a reflection of the many luminous beings—seen and unseen—who have walked with me, touched my heart, and inspired the journey home. I am deeply blessed and grateful.

To **Suzanne Giesemann** who graciously agreed to write the foreword for this book—your wisdom, authenticity, and guidance have shaped my path in profound ways. Thank you for demonstrating how evidence-based spirituality and heartfelt mysticism can walk hand in hand.

To **Eileen Davies** for being a loving example of true humility, loving-kindness, and grace. Thank you for your gentle encouragement to trust in the love and guidance of those in spirit, and for shining so brightly as a testament to what's possible when we live in alignment with Spirit.

To **Sally Hawk** at VerySoul.com—thank you for your soul-centered support and loving presence along the way.

To **Joanna Lake,** my dear cousin—for your willingness to jump in and read this book before publication. Though many miles may separate us physically, we remain ever close in Love.

To **Jack Eleini** for the many conversations, for your humor, your love, and for your steadfast support and encouragement as this journey continued to unfold.

To my **Loving Family**—for without your continued love, support, and encouragement none of this would be possible. I love you.

To you, **the reader**—to all my clients and those who have repeatedly asked, "When are you going to write a book?" Thank you for your inspiration. It is for you that I have written and now share these pages. My heartfelt hope is that within them, you will find inspiration, resonance, and encouragement for your own unique and sacred journey of surrender into love.

With love and deep gratitude,

Tammy Lee Anderson

Foreword by: SUZANNE GIESEMANN

Have you ever used the word "delicious" to describe something you've read? If not, you may be inclined to do so as you immerse yourself in this feast of a book.

Gorge yourself on Tammy's words. Binge read, if you wish, and I dare say you may find that any emptiness inside will fill with the kind of satisfaction we rarely find from human words.

If this sounds like hyperbole, you are about to experience this truth for yourself. There is an energy to this magnificent memoir that led me to crave more each time I set the pages aside to go about my mundane business. This is heavenly prose that will be felt at the soul level. Read slowly and savor every word. Your soul will thank you.

I first met Tammy when she attended my class in mediumship in a hotel ballroom in California. She stood out to me for her unique mix of serenity, shyness, humility, and an underlying "I've got a secret" air that left me cocking my head in curiosity each time I tuned into her distinctive energy.

That secret—as I have come to learn—is that Tammy "gets" who we really are and why we're here. This profound awareness comes with no cockiness or judgment, simply a strong sense of quiet presence that I deeply admire.

As we have interacted over the years, I've never failed to be impressed by Tammy's dedication to whatever task she undertakes, most especially her spiritual journey. As you will discover in this delectable collection of stories, she has an innate desire to be of service in whatever capacity presents itself, and a childlike sense of humor that peeks out from behind a veiled but palpable iron core.

Suffice it to say, Tammy Lee Anderson is one of the most unusual— and admirable—people I have met. I am a spiritual teacher and an author, yet in Tammy's presence, I maintain what she would know as "beginner's cup." She stands as a teacher for me on multiple levels, not the least of which is her dedication to milking this life for all that her soul came here to learn.

We would all be wise to learn from Tammy Lee Anderson.

And that is what you have the chance to do in this astoundingly captivating and lyrical book. You will learn how a near-death experience at birth affected the way Tammy would view the world for the rest of her incarnation. You will see how she consistently took what some might see as negative situations and turned them into opportunities.

You will observe how she came out of the closet—her childhood place of refuge—and turned her hyper-sensitivity into a gift of strength. You will follow her from military bases to monasteries, from quiet solitude to deep, loving relationships that many seek but rarely find, from deep grief to the humble exultation that comes from self-realization.

As I read in the final chapters how Tammy applied her martial arts skills to her current work as a medium, I found myself repeatedly saying, "Yes! Yes!" I could see that she clearly understands that the same skills that she as an Aikido practitioner learned to master and teach to others translates into precisely what is needed for clear and concise transdimensional communication.

Those skills are surrender and humility, and Tammy Lee Anderson is the perfect person to teach you about them.

You need not be a medium or a martial arts practitioner to benefit from *Into Love*. This book will serve any student of life well, modeling the skills that we as souls came here to master.

I am honored to call Tammy Lee Anderson my friend as well as my spiritual teacher. I honor you as well for following your soul's nudge to read this book. You will soon understand why I am so excited about the delicious feast you are about to enjoy.

Suzanne Giesemann, Author of *The Awakened Way*

INTRODUCTION

"A true teacher is transparent, allowing divine presence to flow through and creates the conditions for others to know this presence within themselves."

That first fragile crossing—a premature body slipping between worlds —etched surrender within me as a silent knowing. Not defeat, but a yielding to something vast, to a love I know as home.

This book traces that thread of knowing—how it wove through near-death awakenings, a childhood tuned to unseen frequencies, and the refuge I found in stillness, through military defiance and decades of seeking in monasteries, dojos, and spirit's silent call. These experiences form not a straight path but a mosaic, each story a facet of a life surrendered to love's embrace.

Surrender, as I've come to know it, isn't giving up—it's giving in: a conscious choice to flow with life rather than fight its currents. In the chapel, a priest's prayer at seventeen unlocked memories of infant crossings. In the dojo, Aikido taught me to blend rather than resist. In stillness, I step aside so Spirit may speak. Each moment reveals the same truth: release control and grace arises.

These early near-death memories returned not as vague impressions but as vivid, multisensory experiences—later confirmed by my family's stories. What I had never been told, I had lived twice: once in infancy, and again in remembrance.

My spiritual awareness arose not from teachings but from direct experience—a pull toward the unseen, a knowing beyond words. What began in that cradle of memory became a life of spiritual discovery and surrender.

Why does surrender matter in a world that prizes strength and certainty? I wondered that too, especially during times of profound loss —my brother's sudden departure, a lover's quiet farewell—when grief left me raw and reaching. Yet each time I let go, something enduring remained: a Love that persists beyond endings, a connection that defies separation.

Through paddling a kayak against the tide, offering healing to a friend across continents, sketching a face I've never seen, I've discovered that surrender isn't passive. It's a fierce softness—a willingness to trust what lies beyond sight.

This is my offering: these pages offer you that same open space—an invitation to pause, to listen, and to recognize the sacred within your own story. A life laid bare not to explain but to resonate—with you, with mystery, with the Love that holds us all. May these pages echo what already lives within you—a golden thread, a quiet remembrance, the pulse of a love that has always been yours.

PART I

Remembering

REMEMBERING THE LIGHT

" What the soul remembers, the mind has never known—and in that remembering, we find our way home. "

I was just seventeen when the boundaries between past and present dissolved in a moment of unexpected grace, awakening memories from before my first breath. Until then, I carried an unspoken longing—a yearning for something unseen.

Near my home stood a chapel, its old stones exhaling the soft scent of incense, where candle flames danced gently, casting soft shadows into stillness. For months, it beckoned me. I would walk past, feeling its quiet call, as though those weathered stones held memories I had yet to remember. Within its embrace, I recognized the voice of my childhood longing—an ache for realms beyond, woven softly through my days.

My family hadn't raised me in any formal faith tradition; they were good, honest people whose morality needed no church pews to flourish. Yet something drew me to that sacred space. I would slip inside, sitting quietly in the back, letting the stillness wash over me. Sunlight streamed through stained glass, painting patterns of jeweled light across the stone floor—whispering in a language I almost understood, fragments of truth hovering just beyond reach. The scent of beeswax candles and aged wood became a comfort, a sensory bridge to something timeless.

Since childhood, a silent weight had shadowed my heart—a sorrow I couldn't articulate, its roots hidden in the fragile crossings of my premature birth and early brushes with death. It was a quiet ache, wordless yet profound, that made the chapel's stillness feel like a refuge.

For weeks, I had noticed a priest in the chapel—sometimes quietly cleaning, adjusting a candle, or smoothing the large cloth that covered the stone altar. Other times, he simply sat in stillness, lost in silent prayer. Our interactions were limited to respectful nods—he acknowledging my presence, me grateful for his silence. This priest seemed to understand that some journeys require space, stillness, and time.

One afternoon, the priest approached me, his kind eyes reflecting genuine curiosity rather than expectation. "I've noticed you sitting here often," he said softly, settling beside me on the wooden pew. "What draws you to this chapel?"

I struggled to articulate what I had no words for. "I'm not sure exactly," I admitted. "Something in the silence... it speaks to me."

He nodded as if he understood. "Would you like me to offer a prayer?" he asked, his voice gentle, his tone making it clear I could decline.

When I agreed, I expected words—formal phrases from liturgy, perhaps. Instead, he asked me to close my eyes, placed his hands lightly on my head, and sank into a deep silence.

At first, nothing seemed to happen. Then came a warmth—not like sunshine or a heater's glow, but something that began to rise from within and spread outward. It flowed from the crown of my head, down through my shoulders and chest, settling in the pit of my stomach. My breathing slowed, as though time itself had thickened around me.

Then, like a film reel set in motion, images and sensations cascaded through me—not seen with my eyes but felt with my entire being. I felt the womb's embrace, the pressure of birth, and fears that weren't mine, yet somehow were. In this expanded state of awareness, I relived memories of floating in radiant light, immersed in boundless peace—moments when my awareness hovered between life and death. Emotions too complex for an infant, somehow recorded in the cellular memory of my body. These weren't vague impressions but vivid knowings—as real as the wooden pew beneath me and the scent of candle wax in the air.

What overwhelmed me most were the emotions that flooded through—not just wonder, or peace, but complex emotions that felt shared between my mother and me: fear, shame, worry, and a desperate desire not to disappoint someone deeply loved.

I realized in that moment a truth that would later find voice in Thich Nhat Hanh's teachings—that we are a continuation; the seeds of my mother's emotions had been planted deep in the soil of my consciousness. Her shame had become my shame, her guilt my guilt. Throughout my young life, I had carried an inexplicable feeling that I had somehow caused pain for my parents simply by being born, though I had never understood the source of this burden until that silent prayer. In that moment, I understood that the ache I had carried was never mine alone—but a thread woven through generations, holding both sorrow and love in its strands.

Time dissolved as I sank into a deep peace, my awareness lifting into a space of light and clarity. When the prayer ended, I knew with absolute certainty that what I had experienced was real—more real than ordinary reality, more vivid than any memory. These were not mere memories but experiences I fully relived.

Yet I needed to speak with my mother—not to validate what I already knew, but to see if my experience matched a history I had never been told.

Days later, I sat with my mother in the bright-orange delivery van she drove for my parents' drapery business. The close quarters of the van created an unexpected sanctuary for what I needed to share.

"Mom, something happened during that prayer," I began softly. "I experienced things—feelings, moments from before I could possibly remember."

As I described the cascade of emotions and impressions—fears I couldn't have known, feelings that weren't mine and yet somehow were —her hands tightened around the steering wheel, though we weren't moving. Tears began to stream down her face, silent and steady.

"How could you know?" she whispered. "We never told you any of this."

In her tears, I found not just confirmation, but an invitation to understand the story of my beginning—a profound realization that we carry far more within us than our conscious minds can explain. What I had held within me was not mine alone—it was a sorrow and a love passed down, woven through the tapestry of generations.

Later, when we were ready, she shared the full story—a chapter of my beginning that she quietly held all my life. My father had grown up in San Francisco, a latchkey child before the term existed. As the son of hardworking immigrants—my grandmother from Palermo, Sicily, and my grandfather from Guadalajara, Mexico—he was left to his own devices from a startling young age. By six or seven, he was running unsupervised through the streets—playing in railroad yards, sneaking into the Cow Palace arena, learning to be self-sufficient in ways most children never need to be. With few rules and little oversight, he grew into a wild, independent young man.

My mother, by contrast, was raised in the quiet town of Ojai, California, by conservative parents who instilled in her a deep sense of responsibility. Her father, my grandfather, had been the city gardener for forty years—a steady, good-hearted man she never wanted to disappoint. My parents met at the orange packing house where they both worked alongside my maternal grandmother, filling crates with California oranges for market.

She recounted how my father's friend bet him one dollar that he couldn't get anywhere with the 'goody-two-shoes' girl—the virtuous type who followed all the rules. My father, never one to back down from a challenge, persisted until she agreed to a date.

She told me about their first date—her first time ever stepping into a restaurant. As the two of them walked through the door, people naturally glanced up. Overcome with shyness, she backed up a few steps, then turned and retreated to the safety of the car.

My father, unfazed, simply said, "I'll be back after I get some dinner," and left her to decide whether to join him. Eventually, she gathered her courage and went inside. "After that, as my father would later joke, he couldn't keep her away from restaurants—'and it cost me a pretty penny,' he'd say, grinning."

Their dating led to Lovers' Lane, beneath the cross that stands high on a hill overlooking the city of Ventura and the sea below. It was there I was conceived, in the back of a red 1955 Ford Fairlane. My father won his dollar, but the bet soon brought unexpected consequences when my mother discovered she was pregnant.

She described the fear of disappointing her beloved father, whose approval meant everything to her. Marriage hadn't been in their immediate plans, but my unexpected arrival changed everything—a truth lovingly protected throughout my childhood.

Yet what began with a trivial bet had endured. More than sixty-three years later, they are still going strong—both now in their eighties, enjoying life together.

Understanding this history helped me see how the emotions I had experienced in that chapel prayer were woven through my parents' history. That chapel moment at seventeen became a pivotal awakening —a doorway to remembering what had always stirred within. Even as a child, I had felt it in the quiet, a pull to the unseen.

Classical music had become my sanctuary early in life. While the rest of my family had little interest in Mozart or Beethoven, I would spend hours in my bedroom, eyes closed to the world yet open to the melodies that enveloped me. Something in those complex harmonies resonated with that part of me that had always sensed more than I could see.

As the melodies wove themselves through the stillness, I found myself slipping into the spaces between the notes. It wasn't just listening; it was a form of transport—as if the music opened doorways to a place I somehow recognized, though I had never been there in this life.

In those moments, the walls of my room seemed to dissolve, and I existed in a vastness that felt more like home than anything in my physical surroundings. My body remained on the bed, but something essential in me expanded beyond it, experiencing a reality that ordinary language couldn't capture.

My father would occasionally comment on my unusual musical tastes—"Why not something normal for a teenager?" he'd ask, half-teasing. He didn't realize that in those compositions, I had found a thread that connected me to a realm I had briefly touched as an infant—a place of light and knowing that existed before and beyond physical form.

I often retreated inward, finding solace in those melodic landscapes, where a presence both intimate and boundless seemed to breathe through the spaces in between. I was a natural contemplative.

The day of the priest's prayer became a turning point—drawing me closer to a presence I had always sensed, a bridge between the seen and unseen realms. In that sacred moment of healing touch, something crystallized within me, threading together fragments of awareness that had long hovered at the edges of my perception.

I yearned to know Love—true, vast, and real—through direct communion with Spirit. What I would understand much later was that I could not *know* Love; I could only experience it. Love is not a matter of the mind, but of the heart and spirit, rising up through the human experience. Love is not something to find, but to remember—a remembering of our true essence.

I now believe this longing was born of those earliest encounters with death as an infant, when I had touched a realm of pure Love only to be called back to physical life. The struggle wasn't intellectual but of a heart that felt lost and longed for reunion with its beloved.

In that moment of the priest's prayer, the veil thinned, allowing me to remember what had always been present—quiet, patient, waiting. I would come to understand there was never any need to reach for what had never left me—what had always lived within.

This first surrender opened a door that would lead to many others —each one revealing that true strength doesn't come from controlling life, but from yielding to the rhythm of something vaster than myself. It was the beginning of understanding that the path I would walk wasn't about escaping the world, but about discovering how deeply I belonged to it—and to the Love that pulses through everything.

Soon after that chapel experience—after the priest's prayer awakened a deep remembering within me—I converted to Catholicism, seeking a path to deepen the connection I had felt in that sacred moment. A Spiritualist church might have called to me just as easily, had one stood nearby. The rituals gave form to what I had only sensed in silence. The incense, the chants, the ancient words—they were outward echoes of an inner knowing, landmarks on a map I was just beginning to read.

Thoughts of a religious community stirred—a life of silence and prayer to hold my longing for Love's embrace. The monastic life beckoned with its rhythm of contemplation and service, a form that might contain the vastness I had glimpsed.

That seed blossomed into theological and philosophical studies—a path nourished by that chapel gift and guided by a quiet hunger to understand. I devoured the mystics—Teresa of Avila, John of the Cross, Thomas Merton—discovering in their words echoes of truths I had touched in silence.

Their language of darkness and light, of knowing beyond knowing, gave voice to what had long lived within me. Yet even as I studied their maps, I sensed my journey would follow paths uniquely mine.

What I remembered that day through the priest's healing prayer may stretch belief, but it remains as real to me as my breath. There was no voice from above—just a profound remembering, a veil briefly lifted to reveal what had always been there.

I remembered a love that preceded my birth, a belonging that transcended this life. It was not a memory of events but of essence—a knowing that ran deeper than thought. Among these memories were glimpses of experiences that seemed impossible—sensations of floating in radiant light, immersed in boundless peace during those early brushes with death as an infant. These glimpses would later reveal themselves as part of a larger truth—that consciousness extends beyond the boundaries of physical form, with human life as one of its many radiant expressions.

PERHAPS YOU'VE FELT it too—a sudden knowing, a silent recognition that feels undeniably true. A moment when something ordinary—a sunset, a child's laugh, a strain of music—briefly becomes a window into the infinite.

That is how I offer this story: as a quiet invitation to notice those moments when the eternal brushes against time in your own life.

The warmth lingered as I stepped outside. The world felt sharper—birds calling, leaves rustling—yet I carried a stillness within, a quiet glow from that sacred prayer. Colors appeared more vivid, sounds clearer, as if my senses had been tuned to a finer frequency.

People passing on the sidewalk appeared luminous in their ordinariness, each face a singular expression of something universal.

It was not about explanation; it was about seeing. Every step, every ache, tied to a Love I knew before breath. The doubts and questions that had once plagued my teenage mind didn't vanish—they simply found their place in a larger context. The intellectual wrestling with faith and meaning continued, but now it was grounded in an experience that reason alone could neither give nor take away.

That moment in the chapel would become just one of many surrenders—each one teaching me that true power flows not from control, but from yielding to something greater. The path ahead would wind through deserts and dojos, across mountains and rivers, circling always back to the same truth: when we loosen our grip on how things should be, we open ourselves to Love's infinite possibility.

The gift of a priest's healing prayer became a doorway—not to escape the world, but to discover how deeply I belonged to it, and to the Love that pulses through everything. The longing I had carried did not signify absence, but a remembered belonging so vast it could never truly be lost.

INVITATION TO PAUSE

- Have you ever experienced a moment when the boundaries between past and present dissolved, revealing something you somehow already knew? What memories or knowings live within you that feel older than your conscious experience?
- Consider the places that call to you—perhaps a church, a forest, a quiet room. What draws you there? What is your soul seeking in those sacred spaces?
- Take a moment to reflect on the emotions or burdens you've carried that might not entirely be your own. How might understanding the threads that connect you to previous generations bring both healing and compassion?
- When has silence spoken to you more clearly than words? What would it mean to trust those wordless knowings that arise from the depths of your being?
- What would change in your life if you fully believed that the love you're seeking has always been within you?

A WARRIOR'S FIRST BREATH

"Every wound becomes a doorway when we let Love in."

Every life begins with a breath, yet mine unfolded like a warrior stepping onto a battlefield. At just seventeen, a chapel prayer unlocked buried memories—not just of my birth, but of multiple death experiences, crossings that shaped me from my earliest days. These memories flooded through me—feelings, sensations, sounds, and images I had carried without knowing, revealed in vivid detail.

I arrived two months early, a fragile 4.3-pound form, later dropping to only 3.3 pounds. My mother, just nineteen, bit down on her own hand, determined not to make a sound, her silence steadied by my grandmother's urging to be strong. That fierce thread was woven into me, a legacy of quiet courage I embody still. After thirty-eight grueling hours, the doctors pronounced me stillborn, the umbilical cord coiled tight around my neck. They carried my blue form to another room, their hands working urgently to bring me back.

The hospital room dissolved and I floated in a radiant sea, embraced by golden light. In that silence, surrender lingered near, too tender to grasp. I could feel my mother's silent call willing me to return, her prayer a beacon guiding me back. I saw her face—young, exhausted, her dark hair damp with effort. She held on without a cry, and that holding became a tether. My breath came, slow and small, a gift born of that stillness.

But my journey beyond the veil was not finished. Six months later, my skull's sutures had closed too soon—a condition called craniosynostosis. Without space to grow, the skull pressed dangerously against my fragile brain. It was a silent danger my parents faced, their hearts full of love and fear. Two skilled surgeons arrived at our hospital to present a new procedure for children with my exact condition—there by chance, or guided by something more. My parents said yes to the risky procedure, trusting it as my only hope. Their courage became another quiet thread, stitching me ever closer to life.

When the day of the first surgery arrived, the anesthesia overwhelmed my small body, stopping my heart. Once again, I left my form behind and was lifted into a Love so vast it held no limits. Beings of light surrounded me, their presence warm and familiar. Joy filled me—a freedom so complete I felt no need to return. The operating room faded, its sounds a soft hum against Love's calm embrace. I rested in that quiet, tasting a Love without end, until a sudden jolt pulled me down. Cold brushed my skin; harsh lights burned my eyes. I did not want to return—the shift from boundless peace to overwhelming fear.

The doctor stepped out, his face pale, telling my parents, "We almost lost her." Their world stopped. Hearts froze. Time slowed. Days later, they took me home—to recover, to gain weight, to grow stronger. Those weeks blur in my memory, like a soft veil. My mother later shared them with me, her voice heavy: "You would lie calm and peaceful one moment, then without warning cry out in screams, as pressure swelled in your head." She held me close, her hands trembling against my skin, her whispers a steady lifeline through those storms, urging me to hold on.

Two months later, the day of the second surgery arrived. The team adjusted the anesthesia, guarding my heart, and this time I stayed, awake to every pulse. Cold touched my skin. Lights glared. Antiseptic caught my breath. Tubes pressed into my throat, and I quivered—jaw shaking, body gripped by primal fear. Sounds rang: metal's clink, a saw's hum cutting bone, the crack of my skull parting. Pain rose, real and fierce, my throat constricted, and I felt like I couldn't breathe. Yet in an instant, the experience transformed. Amid that storm, a healing light flowed— soft, steady, guiding the surgeons' hands. Like a warrior finding calm in battle's chaos, I existed in two places at once—here, in my body, and there, in the light where all struggle dissolves. Surrender was not escape; it was trust—allowing the light to hold me through the fear. I could not cry—my voice was gone—but I felt it all, knowing Love's steady presence.

These warrior beginnings left their mark—a quiet strength that flows through me still. When I later shared this recollection with my mother, her tears fell, her voice barely a whisper: "I didn't let you go." That early peace, tucked deep within me, became a seed waiting to blossom into awareness. My life began not with a cry, but with a surrender—not to struggle, but to a love that is always there.

I don't know why these memories remain so vivid—that space in between, that quiet where light rests within me, more real than the dawn outside my window. Perhaps you've known it too, a knowing without words. This presence flows through me like a warrior's steady breath—a current carrying me through both life's battles and its moments of grace. Not bold or dramatic, but persistent and sure, like water finding its way through stone.

Over the years, humor has become an essential companion. When I have my hair cut, beauticians often notice the scars on my head and ask what happened. I joke, saying, "All my marbles fell out, and the doctors had to perform emergency surgery to put them back in. I think they might have missed one or two."

This ability to find lightness in the presence of my scars has been its own form of healing—a way of honoring the journey without being defined by it.

That passage between worlds has shaped not just my spiritual path, but also how I navigate everyday life—with lightness, even when reminders of those early struggles arise. What began as a fragile breath blossomed into a life guided by the steady light of Love.

Looking back, I see the threads of my life intertwining—each moment revealing a deeper essence of who I am. The warrior's breath, the strength, the moments of surrender, and the Love are not separate parts of me, but aspects that flow together, forming the whole.

Each step, each turn, has led me here. I am grateful for all of it—for how it has shaped me into who I am today. A golden thread of Love sustains me through storms and illuminates quiet moments, revealing again and again the truth I first knew before taking breath: we are never separate from the Love that flows through us all.

INVITATION TO PAUSE

- Have you ever felt yourself between two worlds—the physical and something beyond? What do those liminal moments reveal about your own relationship with the mystery of existence?
- Consider your own "warrior's breath"—the quiet strength that has carried you through life's most challenging moments. How has adversity shaped the deeper essence of who you are?
- Where in your life have you discovered that surrender is not giving up, but rather trusting something greater than your own understanding?
- Take a moment to reflect on the early imprints of your own life—the struggles, the moments of grace, the threads that were woven before you could even understand them. How

do those beginnings continue to inform who you are becoming?

- What would it mean to embrace both your scars and your healing as equally sacred parts of your journey?

THE SONG WITHIN

*"Every moment of awakening is simply remembering
what your soul never forgot."*

Some children are born with an inner antenna, tuned to frequencies that others might easily filter out—a sensitivity that perceives both beauty and discord with an almost painful clarity. I was one of them. My earliest memories were awash in sensations that both overwhelmed and enchanted me.

Our home thrummed with the voices of at least twenty children my mother cared for—their laughter and cries forming a constant symphony that both animated and exhausted me. Where others heard only noise, I sensed layers: the bright ping of plastic toys colliding, the high pitch of excitement as children burst through our front door, the trembling undertone of tears from those clinging to their parents' legs, the smell of unchanged diapers that made me retreat to the farthest corner of the room. My mother moved through this soundscape with graceful purpose—her gentle voice a steady bass line beneath the chaos.

While she embraced the whirlwind of nurturing twenty young lives, I longed to disappear, my senses perpetually raw and exposed. When the crescendo grew too intense, I would press my palms against my ears and slip outside to the yard, where my small hands found solace in mud—cool, yielding, and blessedly silent. I shaped little bowls with careful fingers, watching their edges crumble under the California sun, learning early lessons in impermanence and creation. The earth spoke a language I understood without words, soothing my curious mind with its quiet knowing.

My grandmother's house offered a different frequency altogether. One Saturday, after an especially overwhelming week, my mother drove me to Grandma's, understanding without words what I needed. There, time stretched like honey—sweet and unhurried. The ticking of her mantel clock, the soft rustle of curtains in the afternoon breeze, the distant chime of church bells—these gentler sounds created a sanctuary where my nervous system could finally exhale.

I would sit beside her, melting into her embrace, simply absorbing the peace of her presence. It didn't matter what her hands were doing—knitting, baking, folding laundry—what mattered was the calm that radiated from her, a steady warmth wrapping around me like a blanket. In her unhurried movements and soft gaze, I found a template for being, one that stood in quiet contrast to the frenetic pace of our bustling home.

Our front yard's massive plum tree became my first temple. I'd scramble up its trunk with the fearless determination only a child possesses, settling into the crook of a branch shaped perfectly for my small form. From that perch, the world transformed—the neighborhood sounds softened into a distant hum, the breeze whispering through leaves that seemed to speak directly to me. I'd pluck the ripest plums, their juice staining my hands and chin as I bit into their sweetness—a quiet communion. Sometimes I stayed until twilight painted the sky in watercolors, reluctant to descend from that branch where time slowed and silence cradled me.

Music found me like a divining rod finds water—both inevitable and essential. While other children my age gravitated toward playground rhymes and simple melodies, I was drawn to nuances that bypassed my ears and spoke to something deeper. I listened to the spaces between the sounds, my small hands tracing invisible patterns in the air, as if weaving the notes into tapestries only I could see. The swell of a violin could lift me—weightless—drawn along a thread of light toward a place I had known before breath. In those moments, I disappeared completely into the music, tasting what mystics call ecstasy: the dissolution of self into something vast and holy.

The contrast between my inner and outer worlds became unmistakable in kindergarten. "Tammy is a quiet child. She never says anything," my teacher wrote, capturing the stillness I maintained amid the classroom's chaotic rhythm. The fluorescent lights, the scraping of chairs, the overlapping voices—all of it became a wall of noise that drove me inward, into watchful silence. Yet when we moved to the playground, something shifted. I came alive—a whirl of energy, chasing balls, racing friends, laughing in motion. Sports became a bridge—one that transformed my inner intensity into movement others could meet.

I developed my personal geography of peace—the brick fence between our house and the neighbor's became a tightrope where I practiced balance—of body and of being. I'd run back and forth along it, arms outstretched, thrilled by the risk of falling and the quiet triumph of staying upright. This delicate negotiation between danger and safety, between movement and stillness, between falling and flight, would become a lifelong dance. Even then, something in me was learning to listen—to the edge, to the moment, to the space where aliveness lives.

My sensitivity carried burdens as well as gifts. A door slamming could send me bolting outside, my heart racing with a fight-or-flight response far bigger than the moment seemed to warrant. Loud voices pierced me like physical blows, and the emotional undercurrents in a room would wash over me like tidal waves, leaving me disoriented and drained. I didn't have words for this experience then—only the sense that I was too porous, too easily flooded by what others could ignore. I didn't yet know that my nervous system was more finely tuned, registering signals that others had learned to filter out.

One crystalline afternoon, perched atop that fence with a plum pit in my hand, a moment of awareness descended—gentle but unmistakable. As I studied the pit in my palm, time stretched thin, revealing how this small seed contained an entire future of shade, blossoms, and fruit —my first lesson in how the infinite often hides within the ordinary. Something opened in my chest, a knowing beyond words, connecting the plum, the tree, the sky, and me in a quiet web of belonging. I didn't speak of it to anyone; some experiences resist language, especially in a world so loud with motion.

While these moments of clarity remained private treasures, my outer world continued its ebb and flow. My mother saw it all—my whirlwinds and my stillness, my retreats and my exuberance—with the weary wisdom of someone who recognized but couldn't quite name what made her daughter different. "You feel everything so deeply. You take everything to heart," she would say—a simple acknowledgment that affirmed my experience, even if she couldn't fully understand its scope.

These tender years shaped me—a will to explore paired with a need for sanctuary, curiosity balanced by contemplation. What once appeared as a contradiction was, in truth, a harmony of complementary forces, teaching me to dance between worlds. The sensitivity that sometimes felt like a burden in childhood would later become my greatest strength: in Aikido's responsive flow, the intuitive touch of healing hands, and the receptive stillness of listening to those in realms unseen.

That song within me—first heard in mud-bowls and plum branches —was a thread connecting me to a Love beyond form. It wasn't about escaping noise, but about learning to discern which sounds carried meaning, and how to rest in stillness amid the storms. It wasn't about slowing down, but about being fully present—to wonder, to beauty, to the sacred disguised as the ordinary. In those early days, I learned my first lessons in surrender: yielding to the music's call, to the tree's embrace, to moments of unexpected knowing—without resisting the world's intensity or my own nature. I began to discover how to rest in unanswered questions, how to find home in the spaces between certainties—an inner harmony that would continue unfolding through every chapter ahead.

INVITATION TO PAUSE

- What were the sacred spaces of your own childhood? Where did you go when the world felt too loud, too bright, or too overwhelming?
- Consider your own inner antenna—what frequencies do you naturally attune to that others might miss? How has this sensitivity served as both gift and challenge in your life?
- Recall a moment from childhood when you felt connected to something larger than yourself—perhaps through nature, music, or quiet solitude. What did that experience teach you about your soul's deeper knowing?
- Where do you still seek that balance between stimulation and sanctuary, between engaging with the world and retreating into your own inner temple?
- How might honoring your sensitivity—rather than seeing it as something to overcome—transform your relationship with yourself and the world around you?

PART II

Sensitivity's Thread

PREFACE TO PART II

From my earliest memories, a thread of knowing wove through me—both gift and weight—drawing me to witness what others couldn't see. This sensitivity pierced time's veil, revealing glimpses of passing souls, whispered farewells, and Love that transcends endings. It arrived without warning—my grandfather's approaching transition, a child named Cassie I had never met, my brother's final goodbye—each perception a burden I couldn't carry, yet ultimately became a light that illuminated deeper truths.

These stories trace my journey through this sensitivity—from a quiet child seeking refuge in silent spaces, to a teenage athlete finding peace on water's mirror, to a sister facing unbearable loss. Through each experience, I learned: this thread wasn't meant to change fate. It was meant to invite me to bear witness—to honor transitions with presence, and to find surrender in what cannot be altered.

I share these experiences to honor what endures—they are reflections of a heart learning to release and still love. These moments taught me to recognize the luminous stillness that awaits when we let go of what must pass—to trust that love persists, even beyond endings.

Perhaps in these stories, you'll glimpse threads of your own sensitivity—those moments when something deeper than reason whispered truths your mind could not grasp, yet your heart instinctively recognized.

TENDER YEARS

"Sensitivity is not weakness,
it is the soul's way of listening deeply to life."

As a child, I carried a quiet strength—a thread woven deep from my earliest battles, a will that held me through birth's fragile crossing. Born premature, I arrived tender to a world too loud, too bright, too sharp.

Noises jolted me—a slammed door, a raised voice—while lights and smells pressed close. I sought refuge in the small closet, a haven where dust hung heavy and the woolen scent of my father's winter jacket wrapped around me like a prayer.

Knees drawn up, I sat, feeling my heartbeat slow—a rhythm steadying me when the outside grew vast. That was my first lesson in surrender—though I had no words for it then.

My father, a man of strong spirit and firm ways, filled our home with a presence I could not escape. The sharp scent of pine aftershave announced him before his footsteps. "You are too sensitive," he would say—his voice firm, his rough hand brushing my hair—a touch that landed deep on my young heart. It stung like criticism, a fault I couldn't fix. I shrank beneath it, my wide-open senses catching every edge.

I love him deeply, knowing he meant no wound. Our bond was forged through those storms—a gift I would not trade. They shaped me: strong-willed, yet open, molded by struggle into someone both resilient and tender.

My mother balanced him. Her quiet was a soft anchor. She saw my need for silence, letting me linger in that small closet unquestioned— her gentle eyes a steady light. The cool silk of her palm against my cheek spoke love without words.

I did not understand why I felt so much—why every emotion flowed into me so intense and raw. That sensitivity, born of my early crossings—birth, surgery—left me open, a river without banks.

At seven, I sat by our house, watching mourners stream into our neighbor's home. Their son, eighteen, had died in a motorcycle accident. I didn't know him, but the sorrow in the air felt like it belonged to me. Their grief sank into me—wordless, heavy, raw.

I wondered what it was like to lose someone so loved—a mystery I couldn't yet grasp. But something in me knew it mattered. That sorrow had shape, and it entered me. Years later, when my brother, also eighteen, died in a car accident, I would understand.

Crossing the grass, I felt a pang—my steps bent blades of green and crushed a beetle. Harm without intent. Even small steps could wound.

So much pain in the world, I thought, even in my small presence. I resolved then to bring as much good as I could. To tread lightly. To lessen the hurt. It was a child's vow, but it took root. Quietly. Completely.

Around that same time, one of my goldfish died. Most were given an unceremonious farewell—the flush of a toilet, the swirl of water carrying them away. But this time, I felt it wasn't enough. The little fish had brought me joy. It deserved something more.

My mother sensed the weight of my request and said yes. I carried the small, still body into the backyard, cradled in a paper towel. I didn't really know how to pray, but I tried. I thanked my little friend.

Then, with muddy hands, I shaped a tiny clay pot—just like the ones I used to make. I placed the fish inside and buried it beneath the plum tree I loved so much. The same tree that held me.

Even then, something in me understood: every life matters. Every ending wants to be seen.

As a teenager, I would lie in my room, playing classical music. I found myself floating between the notes, in the spaces where sound softened into silence. I drifted in that space, touching something gentle—a whisper I had known before my first breath.

One summer, at sixteen, I stepped into a palm reader's tent at the county fair. The air was thick with the scent of cotton candy and warm dust. Inside, it was dim and hushed—a strange kind of stillness beneath the noise of the world.

She smelled of old cigarettes, her voice raspy from the years of inhaling smoke. Yet her eyes—deep green-blue—sparkled when they met mine.

She traced the lines of my palm with a feather-light touch, her fingers steady. "Your will flows like a mighty river," she said, her voice both rough and kind. "There's a force in you—unyielding, strong." She paused for a moment, her gaze resting on something beyond the lines.

"And it carries more than you yet understand."

Her words sank deep—a truth felt but ungrasped, a river I would learn was both blessing and burden.

That river met storms—my father's ways, schoolyard noise—when my will would not bend. I didn't yet know how to soften without losing myself. Back then, surrender felt like not breathing—as if yielding meant disappearing. But in the hush of the small closet, I found a different kind of strength. A stillness that softened the sting.

It would take years before I understood what that palm reader had seen in my hands—what that mighty river truly carried.

Years later, a letter arrived from Arthur Findlay College, a school for spiritual mediumship in the UK. The salutation read: Dear Sensitive, Welcome.

Those words turned a wound into treasure. My sensitivity—once named a flaw—was now recognized as a gift. A gift planted by my mother's silent courage at my birth.

Today, in meditation, I return to that small closet. Once an escape, it is now a sacred space—a space within, where images, impressions, and gentle knowings surface—offered in love.

In surrendering to that river—acknowledged by my father, blessed by the palm reader, cradled by music's silence—I found Love's embrace, where tenderness and strength move not in opposition, but as one.

INVITATION TO PAUSE

- What were your earliest refuges—the spaces where you went when the world felt too overwhelming? How do those childhood sanctuaries continue to inform your need for solitude and restoration?
- Consider your own sensitivity as a child. Was it seen as a gift or a burden? How has your relationship with your sensitive nature evolved over time?
- Recall a moment when you felt compelled to honor something small—a pet, a plant, a simple act of reverence. What did that impulse teach you about the sacredness of all life?
- Where in your life do you still struggle between standing strong in your will and learning to soften without losing yourself?
- How might embracing your sensitivity as a "mighty river" rather than a flaw transform the way you navigate both your inner world and your relationships with others?

PAPA'S LIGHT

"Those we have loved are never truly gone; they live on in the landscape of our hearts, their essence woven into who we become."

At sixteen, I walked beside my grandfather—we called him Papa—after a Thanksgiving feast, just the two of us tracing a quiet path near home. A hard-working man, he had tended the city's gardens as head gardener for forty years, his strong hands outpacing younger men with a pride he wore like a badge. At home, he fixed old watches and clocks—a hobby of patience, coaxing tiny gears until they ticked anew.

That day, as we walked, a heaviness touched my soul—a shift in his energy, carrying with it a wordless awareness of his approaching good-bye. This sensitivity had been with me since childhood—an awareness I once called unfortunate, for sensing loss before it arrives weighs heavily on the heart. I said nothing, unwilling to voice his nearing end, even to myself.

Months later, at a family gathering, a seizure struck—foam at his mouth, his heart stilled briefly. Paramedics revived him as we watched, stunned, frozen, our hearts gripped by fear that we might lose him.

He awoke with a grin. "Well, if that's dying," he said, "it sure is easy!" Then, softer, more to himself than to us, "We are in for it now."

That moment stretched his time, and nearly a year after my Thanksgiving knowing, Papa passed. My family converted our garage into a hospital room, tending him with devoted love—meals, care, presence— until his final breath.

I was not there. The National Championships in kayaking had called me away—a journey shaped by both water and will.

As I paddled, a shadow crossed my heart—I knew Papa had gone. Tears welled. I called home from the camp payphone, sobbing, "I know he is gone." My family had planned to wait, shielding me until I returned, but awareness surged through me—a tide I could not stem. They confirmed it—he had slipped away, his labor done.

I walked slowly back through the campground, tears streaming, the world around me muted by grief. The campground where we stayed for the competition was quiet—tents scattered beneath tall trees, the air still. I crawled into mine and stayed there most of the afternoon, curled into my sadness. My coach checked in now and then, gently pulling back the flap. I couldn't speak. I just turned away. There were no words —only the ache, my Papa was gone.

As the competitions resumed the next day, I moved in a haze—half there, half not. It was my first experience of someone close to me passing. I wondered where he was. It seemed impossible that he could just be... gone. Would I see him again somehow? What happens when someone dies?

These questions drifted in and out of my awareness, like waves moving through fog, rising between the ache of grief and the quiet pull to keep racing. The river called me back to movement, even as part of me longed to be still.

DAYS LATER, a quiet wonder stirred. An old mantel clock at my uncle's house—one he and Papa had tinkered with but left silent for want of parts—began to chime with a tone as familiar as Papa's voice.

The sound stopped my uncle mid-conversation. It filled the room, clear and unexpected, like a breath taken by the house itself. We stood wide-eyed with wonder. No one had touched it. No one had wound it. For three days after his passing, it sounded—a gentle echo of his spirit, soft as his smile, steady as his hands. A presence made audible. A love unbroken by time.

That quiet awareness stayed with me—rising again before my brother's death, and others that followed. Each time, it stirred something deep and familiar, as if part of me remembered what was coming. The feeling is heavy, and often it feels as though I'm going away—as if my own death is near. In some way, that's true. A part of me will always be with them.

At sixteen, Papa's passing left a question lingering: why feel what I cannot shift? Yet in that quiet ache, I found surrender—not to change his path, but to stand with it, offering love where words faltered. Through his clocks—and his ease, that simple "it sure is easy"—I learned that love persists: a light no darkness can dim. I could not keep him here, but I could trust the unseen hands of Love's design to carry him home.

Like Papa's clocks, life ticks in mysterious rhythms—marking time beyond our control. His passing taught me that our souls keep time to a different measure than our bodies, continuing to chime long after their physical gears have stilled.

Those three days of unexpected chimes were more than chance; they were reminders that love's clockwork endures, beyond the hands we see.

My sensitivity to these crossings became a kind of inner timepiece—marking what endures rather than what fades.

When I surrender to this awareness, I find myself standing in a timelessness where Papa's smile still shines, where love's pendulum swings without ceasing, where spirit outlasts flesh's fragile gears.

INVITATION TO PAUSE

- Have you ever sensed a loss before it happened—felt that subtle shift in energy that whispers of coming change? How do you hold space for such knowing when it arrives uninvited?
- Reflect on someone dear to you who has passed. What signs or synchronicities appeared after their transition that felt like messages of their continued presence?
- When grief has called you away from the world, what has eventually drawn you back into movement and engagement? How do you honor both the need to retreat and the call to continue?
- Consider the "clockwork" of your own life—the mysterious rhythms and timing that seem beyond your control. Where have you learned to trust in love's design even when you cannot understand it?
- What would it mean to see your sensitivity to loss not as a burden, but as a sacred ability to stand witness to the eternal nature of love itself?

CASSIE'S LIGHT

"Some lives touch us only for a moment—and transform us forever."

In the quiet of a peaceful morning, a vision slipped into my awareness—unbidden, yet clear as dawn.

I was seventeen, sitting alone outside a prayer room, waiting for a priest friend—a healer whose sessions I often supported. He was inside, offering healing prayer, and I had chosen to join him silently, holding space for whoever was receiving it.

Then, a presence brushed my awareness: a young girl—seven or eight—surrounded by a brilliant light. I had never seen her before, except in this moment of knowing. She told me her name—Cassie—and made me aware that her time here was drawing to a close.

She held her father's hand. His presence felt near, protective, reverent. It was no daydream, but a precognitive awareness I had carried since childhood—a sensitivity I knew well.

I had felt such partings before—my grandfather's fate at sixteen, a girl lost in a farmhouse fire—yet this one came gently, like a hand placed on mine.

It was not a summons to intervene, but an invitation to witness. I spoke no warning. Instead, I offered a silent prayer, a breath of love for her crossing, for her family's peace. The priest worked beyond the door while I remained with Cassie's light—trusting her presence, without needing to understand it.

Later that week, I quietly told my sister: "Watch the papers—a little girl named Cassie will be there." She nodded, familiar with these intuitions of mine, and we waited.

A few days passed. Then her name appeared—Cassie, short for Catherine. She had died of illness. Her age and passing were exactly as I had seen. My sister's eyes met mine, wide with wonder. But I felt no triumph—only a quiet ache, a love I had touched but could not carry.

This awareness had been with me for as long as I could remember— a quiet attunement to what stirs just beyond the seen. As a child, I felt spirits near—knowings I could neither halt nor fully share. Each bore a weight, a question: Why see what I cannot shift?

Yet with Cassie, I glimpsed a shift—not in her leaving, but in my holding. I could stand witness, cradling her light as she crossed. It echoed lessons that surrender, not struggle, opens Love's door. I offered her what I could—presence, a prayer—and released the rest.

The priest emerged that day, his session complete, and I said nothing of Cassie. Her story was not mine to tell, her passing not his to bear. Yet her light lingered—a quiet reminder of Love's reach beyond form.

Cassie taught me that even in loss, Love persists—a thread unbroken by time's end. I could not change her path, but I could honor it, trusting in Spirit's quiet weave. Perhaps you have known this too—a glimpse beyond ordinary sight, a knowing that transcends ordinary perception.

For me, Cassie's visitation transformed sensitivity's burden into surrender's grace—a call to bear witness where words fall short, to offer presence where action cannot reach. In those moments of quiet attunement, I discovered not merely foreknowledge, but participation in a mystery larger than myself.

Beneath that starlit knowing lay not just foretelling, but communion. In that luminous stillness, the boundaries between life and death, known and unknown, dissolve into Love's quiet constancy.

This is the gift I now share with you: That in our deepest listening, we touch what endures beyond time's threshold, holding each other in a light that neither begins nor ends.

INVITATION TO PAUSE

- Have you ever received knowing that came not through your mind, but through a deeper sense of awareness? How did you hold space for such mysterious gifts?
- Consider a time when you were called to simply witness rather than act—to hold space for someone's journey without trying to change their path. What did that teach you about the nature of love and presence?
- Reflect on moments when you've felt touched by the light of someone you barely knew, or knew only briefly. How do such encounters expand your understanding of connection and love?

TWO WATERS

"There is a moment before every wave returns to the sea, a still point,
where tension softens, and what is held...releases.
The wave always knows its way home."

Water has always spoken to me, even in my earliest memories. When I
was just three or four years old, my grandmother would take me to walk
on the pier near our home. I would beg her to take me to what I called
the "Two Waters"—my childhood name for the ocean that flanked both
sides of the wooden walkway. Hand in hand, we ventured out as the
weathered boards creaked beneath our feet. I would pause often,
crouching down to peer through the cracks between the planks,
mesmerized by the waves beneath us. I can still feel the gentle tug of her
hand whenever I lingered too long, watching the hypnotic rhythm
below.

The pier stretched straight out into the vast blue, and we would
walk to the very end, where I'd stand on tiptoe to peer over the edge.
"Two Waters," I would insist, even though my grandmother would

smile and tell me it was all one sea. She eventually started calling it "Two Waters" as well, adopting my child's perspective with loving acceptance. Those walks with my grandmother remain some of my fondest memories. She often came to pick me up and would say, "Let's go to the Two Waters." That simple phrase held a world of connection—a grandmother honoring life through a child's eyes.

There's a quiet kind of wisdom in an adult's willingness to see through a child's eyes. My grandmother could have kept correcting me, insisting on the "proper" view—it was all one ocean. Instead, she stepped into my world, seeing that my perspective wasn't wrong—simply shaped by where I stood and what I could see. In surrendering her adult certainty, she created a bridge between us, teaching me, without words, that love makes space for different ways of seeing the same reality. I find it interesting now—this early perception of one ocean appearing as two, shaped by where I stood. The view depends on where you stand—how point of view shapes experience. Years later, water would call to me again, this time as a path to discover my own strength.

It began with a curious sight—our school coach driving past pulling a 40-foot trailer, kayaks stacked high, their long forms gleaming in the early morning light. Excitement stirred in me—a spark of wonder and will. That's how it began—simple as that. Just a young, eager heart drawn toward an unseen river, with no map, only a feeling. For six years, water became my guide—a silent mirror reflecting the parts of me that found joy in challenge.

Training began early—4:30 a.m., before the world stirred. Shoes laced tight, I ran six miles to the marina—air cold on my cheeks, each breath rising like a chant in the stillness. As the sun rose, the marina's glassy water turned to mirror—sky, boats, and silence reflected in stillness. On my first day, I carried a K1 to the water's edge—seventeen feet of sleek Olympic design—my heart full of anticipation. I stepped in, and it rolled! Quick and cold. Splash! I was under—the freezing water a jolt that snapped me awake.

I had stepped into the boat right beside the dock and immediately rolled—K1's are notoriously tippy. After the initial shock of the cold water, my coach helped me back onto the dock. We both laughed as I stood shivering, soaked to the bone. He held the boat steady for a second attempt. This time, I managed to stay upright—wobbly, but paddling. Wet and trembling, I kept going—the boat still unsteady beneath me, but I was determined to continue. I loved the effort the way it called me to grow—not against anyone, but within.

Some days I'd train for six or seven hours, my breath blending with the paddle's rhythm—K1 alone, K2 and K4 flowing in quiet harmony with teammates. By my late teens, that steady dedication had carried me to gold and silver medals, North American Championships, and races on Olympic courses. In 1980, international politics cut short my Olympic dreams—I had placed 13th in the Olympic Trials, holding hope for 1984, but it wasn't meant to be. The medals weren't the heart of it—they were just markers along a deeper current, a path I followed not for competition, but to uncover my own inner strength.

I was quiet by nature, one who didn't fit so easily among crowds. Athletics gave me a place—one where I could be with others, yet rest in my own stillness. The still water held me quietly, its surface offering not just reflection, but a feeling of something deeper stirring. I'd sprint— lungs full, paddle cutting smooth—and I'd feel it: a peace beyond effort. A whisper from the light I had known as an infant, a memory of love's stillness before my first breath. For me, it was about touching that flow —where will and surrender meet, and water quietly held me steady.

Winter training brought me to the Olympic Training Center, where the air bit cold and water lay still beneath the silent gaze of snow-capped mountains. I'd paddle, my spirit open and alive, each stroke a sacred offering to something within. Those winters linger in my memory—we trained intensely, the water icy and still beneath silence and snow. I'd glide out and lose myself in the rhythm, in the harmony of K4 boats moving as one: a quiet dance of breath and paddle. It was magical, not loud, but soft—like a lesson in being free, the water sharing a calm found in the movement.

The river was never about the destination, but the challenge and growth it offered. Like my grandmother, who knew how to hold both her truth and mine at once—"Two Waters" existing alongside one ocean —I learned to hold seemingly opposite realities: effort and surrender, discipline and flow, strength and softness. Kayak training gave me space —not just from the noise of the world, but from the tension at home, where my father's strength and my will often clashed.

Kayaking became a refuge, a place where I could return to stillness within. He'd say, 'too damn sensitive,' and we'd clash—though my love for him endures, a steady light. What I learned from my grandmother stayed with me: perceptions are determined by one's point of view. The challenges with my father helped shape who I've become. The water was my harbor, a challenge I welcomed, a quiet will from infancy rising with each stroke—a way to breathe beyond the storm.

The kayak taught me love's gentle rhythm—balance, breath, and flow in harmony. I was young, with a determined, passionate fire inside, falling in, getting back up—not counting the falls, but the times I paddled on. The water didn't hurry me; it waited, smooth and patient, until I learned its flow.

Life became more peaceful when I let it be—flowing more easily when I moved with it. The gift wasn't out there in medals or recognition —it lived in the quiet challenge, the peace found within when longing surrendered to a greater stillness. Love flows like water—a gentle current lifting us into its embrace, a whisper of home in every breath, reminding us we're never separate from the Source.

INVITATION TO PAUSE

- What "Two Waters" have you seen in your own life—places where your unique perspective revealed something others might have missed or dismissed? How has honoring your own way of seeing shaped your journey?
- Consider the waters that have called to you—literal or metaphorical. What challenges have you stepped into

without knowing the shore, trusting only the current that drew you forward?

- Reflect on times when physical challenge or discipline became a pathway to inner stillness. How has your body been a teacher in discovering the balance between effort and surrender?
- It is our point of view that determines our experience. How might shifting perspective on a current challenge reveal new possibilities?
- Where in your life do you still need a refuge—a place to return to your own rhythm when the world feels too demanding or overwhelming?

MY BROTHER'S LIGHT

"Some bonds are not broken by death, they are revealed by it.
What the soul remembers, love makes visible"

In the months before my brother's passing, a shadow stirred within me —a weight I could neither name nor shed. He was eighteen, five years my junior, a vibrant soul whose laugh illuminated our home. Yet each time he turned away—his back a silhouette against the world—I felt a visceral knowing that he would soon leave and not return. It was no fleeting unease, but a precognitive thread woven quietly through my life.

This sensitivity had been with me since childhood, but it had grown even more acute after an experience that summer. Just three months earlier, during one of my wilderness retreats, I underwent a profound near-death experience. I share this experience not to persuade, but to bear witness—to the power of Love, to the truth that we are more than these bodies, and that death is not the end.

For over a week, I had been hiking alone in the solitude of the mountains, fasting and praying, seeking deeper communion. That summer brought high temperatures, and my body became dehydrated. Exhausted and feeling sick, I lay down on the ground, and the boundary between body and spirit began to fade. What I experienced then would forever expand my awareness of life and death.

Light enveloped me completely, dissolving all boundaries—a tunnel of infinite expanse where souls, radiating with multicolored brilliance, flowed like a river of light toward a radiance of irresistible Love. No earthly illumination compares to what surrounded me—a Light both impossibly brilliant yet soothingly gentle, loving as a perfect embrace, and magnificent beyond imagining—its current guiding me forward without resistance or will.

As I surrendered to this current of consciousness, a familiar presence drew my attention. My grandfather, who had departed years before, stood before me—vibrantly alive in his luminous essence. *Papa*! This recognition arose not as spoken word but as pure feeling, my soul expanding with indescribable joy. When he turned, our essences merged, connecting in a way no earthly embrace could replicate—a reunion where everything was known between us, nothing hidden, nothing lost.

In this luminous state of communion, questions I had carried throughout my earthly journey surfaced effortlessly, like bubbles rising through clear water. *"What is the true story of Jesus? Have you met him?"* —And before the question fully formed, I found myself gazing into the eyes of Jesus himself—his loving presence rewriting the very fabric of my being.

As I began merging into this all-encompassing Love, a beautiful being of light gently drew me aside. Questions I had carried for so long —about suffering, pain, and the nature of existence—began to rise within me. At first, I voiced them aloud, but soon realized that thought alone was enough, as answers arrived even before my questions fully formed.

Suddenly, sparks of multi-colored light began streaming into my consciousness—each one a complete download of understanding, filling my heart with ecstasy. With each revelation, a profound truth washed over me: All is perfect. This Love transcended anything the earthly experience could convey—so intense, so complete, that human language crumbles in its attempt to describe it.

My communion with that realm ended abruptly—I was pulled back into my body by a sound that pierced the veil between worlds: the distinct whinny of a horse startlingly close to my ear. Its breath warmed my skin as if the animal stood directly beside me, though I would later learn the nearest horse roamed miles away, beyond the next mountain. This mysterious presence—whether physical or spirit messenger—acted as an anchor, drawing me back with irresistible force.

The return journey was not a gentle transition but a painful compression—like sinking through amber, slow and thick. Where moments before I had existed as pure consciousness—weightless and free—I now found myself compressed into density. Each cell protested as awareness returned to a body, the heaviness a painful contrast to spirit's lightness. I grieved the departure from boundless Love as my lungs struggled to remember their purpose, gasping in a realm that suddenly felt foreign.

It was with this heightened awareness that, a month before his accident, my brother and I shared lunch at Casa de Soria, our favorite Mexican restaurant in downtown Ventura. We sat in a booth near the back, nestled in a quiet corner. The clatter of plates, nearby voices, and the scent of refried beans and tacos created a familiar comfort around us.

Something beyond reason compelled me to share my spiritual journey. Though spiritual conversations weren't common in our family, I felt driven to tell him everything about my recent near-death experience in the mountains. My brother listened with remarkable stillness, his gaze unwavering as I recounted encountering our grandfather, meeting Jesus, and experiencing that all-encompassing Love. Not a question interrupted the flow, not a flicker of doubt crossed his face—only presence. When I finished, he looked at me with the clarity of uncluttered faith and said simply, "I believe in God." No doctrine. Just conviction.

"Yes," I replied. "There's much more to all this than what appears to be." He nodded, absorbing my words in silence, neither of us knowing he would soon confirm this truth from beyond.

My brother was a natural athlete. While I trained diligently for 10K races to stay in shape for kayak racing, he would occasionally join me, effortlessly gliding past with ease. Just weeks before he passed, Ektelon Inc., a manufacturer of racquetball equipment, had chosen him for professional sponsorship, and he dreamed of opening a sports club someday. I had begun teaching him a little Aikido; with his instinctive athleticism, he would have mastered it effortlessly.

Just before he passed, he had proudly shown me his new haircut, asking, "Do you like it? She cut it so my hair is just off to the side." Days later, at the funeral home, when asked how he combed his hair, I heard his words echo softly: "just off to the side."

In the weeks after our lunch, my sense of foreboding intensified. This wasn't the first time intuition had whispered of impending loss— glimpses of departures I could neither prevent nor fully articulate. I whispered to our mother, "Every time I see his back, I feel he is leaving us." She grew anxious—trusted my intuitions—and urged him to give up his motorcycle, but neither of us could foresee exactly how or when the thread would snap.

The day arrived veiled in ordinary moments, unremarkable at first glance. He walked toward his motorcycle, helmet forgotten, and I called out with sisterly vigilance, *"Where's your helmet?"* He grinned, shrugged —*"Okay"*—and returned with it, visor up. *"Goodbye, I love you,"* he said, his voice carrying an unmistakable finality that struck me like a physical blow. I stood frozen, held in the silence of knowing, engulfed by a certainty I could not yet articulate. Later, as I sat in our parents' car, we stopped where he met his friend—a sixteen-year-old with a new Porsche, a vehicle too powerful for inexperienced hands. Through the back window, I watched my brother climb into the passenger seat, laughing, and knew it was the last time I would see him alive. A gripping haze descended around me as I sat immobilized, as if time had thickened, unable to speak or act, as though watching a slow-motion film unfold before me.

Hours later, the phone rang at home. I turned to our mother before anyone answered and said, "Ron's dead." The words spilled out unbidden, and her eyes widened in panic, "Why would you say that?" she cried. They had raced through the hills, the car spinning out of control and striking a tree. He died instantly; his friend survived, though injured. Regret gripped me—I should not have spoken before the call—but the knowing had surged forth, an unstoppable tide.

Grief engulfed us completely. Reality became distorted—dreamlike, yet nightmarish. Time seemed to slow. I moved through a haze, bewildered that the world continued as normal: traffic flowing, people conversing, while our world had shattered. Family and friends gathered, their sobs filling our home. I felt strangely detached, observing everything as if from a great distance.

Just days after he passed, a package from Ektelon arrived at my parents' house—equipment for the professional career he would never live to begin. The box remained unopened, its silence louder than words, a tangible reminder of stolen tomorrows that made his absence ache all the more.

Though beneath the crushing sorrow, a quiet recognition whispered —a first hint that love might somehow transcend physical separation— true surrender would take much longer to find root in my heart.

I moved through those first days in a fog, finding myself listening for him in the quiet moments. Days later, he returned. I was alone on the porch when my brother appeared, full-formed, as real as the day he left. My heart leapt, then faltered—open as I was to such encounters, the weight of loss and his sudden presence overwhelmed me. "I cannot bear this now," I gasped, and he vanished, respecting my unreadiness. In that moment, his love honored my boundaries—even across worlds. I wasn't ready. Not yet. And he understood.

That night, he came to me across the threshold between worlds— not in the hazy landscape of dreams, but in a visitation more vivid than waking reality. His presence illuminated the darkness of my grief like sunlight breaking through storm clouds. He laughed—that same unmistakable laugh that had once filled our home—his joy untouched by death's crossing. "You're right about one thing," he said, eyes sparkling with cosmic mischief, "there is more to it than what appears to be." These words—my own returned to me from beyond the veil—created a perfect circle between us, spanning life and death. In that moment, the membrane between worlds felt gossamer-thin. The radiance emanating from his presence wasn't merely light, but pure joy distilled to its essence—a peace so profound it temporarily lifted the crushing weight of my grief like boulders becoming weightless in water. In that sacred moment, I understood our bond had never been merely physical, but soul-deep, and what death had seemingly severed, it had actually transformed into something more luminous and eternal.

In the quiet after his appearance, I returned to a truth I had glimpsed in my own near-death experience: Love is eternal. His visit confirmed what my heart already knew—that the death of the body does not end the bonds between us. Consciousness continues. Love remains.

Yet even with this cosmic reassurance, the human part of me still ached with his absence. I missed his physical presence, his voice across the dinner table, the future we would never share. Dreams that would never come to pass—his professional racquetball career, teaching him more Aikido, the years I would never witness him grow into—left a hollow within me, a space that even spiritual knowing could not completely fill. The grief came in waves, sometimes receding as I felt his continued presence, other times crashing over me with the ache of what might have been, if only things had unfolded differently that day.

He died nine days before my 23rd birthday. The months that followed blurred together until I found myself back at university in February. The initial shock had softened, yet in its place settled a heavier, more persistent ache—one that questioned not just his absence, but my own purpose in remaining. His appearance had opened a door between worlds, but I still stood in this one, learning to walk with both the gift of spiritual knowing and the weight of human loss.

Alone in my dorm room, I knelt on the short brown carpet as fading light from the window cast long shadows across the silent space. In that stillness, grief engulfed me anew. Depression, a shadow I had carried since childhood, deepened into despair. I wrestled with impossible questions—could I have altered his fate? Why him instead of me?

From my first breath in this world, I had never truly been alone—spirit's presence had always enveloped me like a mother's embrace, a constant companion through life's journey. But that day, collapsed on my dorm room floor, I teetered on the precipice of my darkest abyss. I heard spirit's gentle voice whisper through the darkness, "I love you"—those words that had always been my anchor. Yet in that moment, they felt like chains. "Leave me alone," I whispered back, my voice hollow with defeat. "Leave me alone now."

The universe honored my request with terrifying immediacy—the loving presence that had been my lifelong companion vanished completely. What replaced it was beyond darkness, beyond silence—a void so absolute it existed outside space and time itself. No whisper of consciousness, no flicker of light remained—only a stillness more profound than death, a nothingness so complete it felt like the blank canvas before creation itself. Language crumbles at the edge of this memory. Human words cannot contain what exists before existence—this vast, perfect absence that was somehow still aware.

"No, this is not what I want—please come back!" My plea dissolved into the void, not even creating an echo in that absolute stillness. Then, in a moment beyond time, I returned—eternity folding into a single heartbeat, the vast nothingness collapsing around me. I found myself once more on that dorm room floor, trembling not from fear but from revelation. What I had glimpsed wasn't death, but something more primordial—the sacred emptiness that precedes all creation, awaiting the first pulse of divine intention.

In the moment that followed, a question rose—not from outside me, but through every fiber of my being: *"Will you stay for Love?"* It touched something so deep, so true, that I could only weep. How could I answer anything but yes to such a question? *"Yes,"* I whispered through tears. *"I will stay for Love."*

As awareness flooded back, Love's embrace held me anew—not

merely as comfort, but revealed as the fundamental architecture beneath all existence. Tears flowed freely, born not of grief, but of profound recognition. The presence I had known since childhood had never truly abandoned me; it had simply honored my request with perfect compassion. Love—patient and eternal—remained, waiting for me to choose return.

Perhaps you have felt this too—grief so deep, a love lingering beyond sight, defying farewell. For me, his passing wove sensitivity's burden, surrender's grace, and love's fierce permanence into my life. I could not halt his leaving, but in releasing despair, I discovered love's eternal presence—though we may turn away, it remains our truest essence.

As time passed, grief transformed into gratitude for the time we shared. First came the surrender of the heart, accepting the physical absence that could never be filled. Later, I learned to surrender my thoughts—the endless *what ifs* and *could have beens* that kept me bound to regret. This wasn't a single moment but a gradual process, like water smoothing stone. Through this surrender, I discovered that my connection to my brother had not diminished but transformed, growing deeper than what was possible in physical form.

Beyond the ache of loss, I found a peace that transcends understanding—a luminous stillness that lives not just in memory, but in every breath. This is the presence I now offer to you.

Through the cracks that loss carved into my being, light now streams unhindered—illuminating chambers of my soul that remained undiscovered before grief broke them open. My brother's passing revealed itself not as an ending, but as a sacred doorway, teaching me that when we surrender our desperate grip on what we believe life and death should be, we awaken to the breathtaking wonder of what they truly are. His final gift—a confirmation that resonates in every fiber of my being: there is *indeed infinitely more to all of this than what appears to be*. And in that knowing lies not just acceptance, but a profound peace—a luminous certainty that love, once born, transcends death, transforming into something vastly more eternal than we, in our earthly limitations ever imagined.

INVITATION TO PAUSE

- Have you ever experienced a knowing that came not through logic but through your deepest intuition? How do you hold space for such awareness, especially when it carries difficult truths?
- Consider a loss that initially felt like an ending but later revealed itself as a transformation. What did that experience teach you about the nature of love and connection?
- Reflect on times when you've asked for divine presence to leave you alone in your pain. How did love respond to your request, and what did you discover about the patient nature of spiritual support?
- What would it mean to trust that the bonds of love are not broken by physical separation but revealed and transformed by it?
- Where in your life might you be gripping too tightly to how things "should be" instead of surrendering to the deeper truth of what is?

EMBODYING THE ART OF PEACE

"True victory is not in overcoming another,
but in allowing love to transform both."

In the autumn of 1982, as the campus trees shed their leaves, I ventured onto the Aikido mat—an eighteen-year-old philosophy student fulfilling a required Physical Education credit, unaware I was stepping into a lifelong practice. Aikido drew me in—described as a non-competitive martial art, the way of harmony and peace. Philosophy classes filled my days, the lives of Mahatma Gandhi and Martin Luther King Jr. igniting my spirit with their vision of nonviolent action. Aikido resonated—a practice with no enemy, where true victory lay within, blending energy into unity. Between falls and flows on the mat came a deep revelation: harmony originates within the centered self—peace arising from within.

The university dojo stood simple, its tatami mats laid over a polished wooden floor smoothed by countless steps before mine, the air alive with presence. On my first day, I practiced with the instructor, a kind man whose calm moved like a river. As we moved through a basic form, he paused, eyes soft with knowing, and said, "You have a lot of defense in your body." From another, the words might have stung, but his voice carried only curiosity, no harm. I stopped, felt the words settle into my awareness, and recognized their truth. My body held walls—fear and vigilance woven tight from early experiences. Fascinated by his simple observation, I glimpsed how this art might gradually unveil me to myself —not to create a weapon against others, but to soften the tension woven around my own spirit. Thus began a lifelong practice of softening, unfolding over decades.

My first fall came fast. I gripped too hard, resisted too much, and the mat rose to meet me. Breath faltered, but the instructor smiled gently. "Blend, do not clash," he said. "Let it flow." I did not fully grasp it then, but I returned—mornings before light, afternoons after study— allowing harmony to seep into me. Aikido unfolded as a dance, its movements circling energy back to stillness, meeting each force where it stood. Each pivot, each roll, mirrored a deeper call—to align with life's flow, to transform struggle into connection.

As years passed, the mat became my teacher. I have now been practicing Aikido for over forty-three years, earning my fifth-degree black belt after four decades of study. For ten of those years, I taught Aikido and self-defense at the university, deepening my own understanding as I guided students through the same movements that had shaped my life. When students expressed interest in continuing beyond university classes, I knew it was time for the next step. In 2002, I opened Shinzen Dojo—a sacred space whose name can mean 'friendship,' 'goodwill,' or even 'before God.' The Japanese garden outside the dojo greeted all who crossed its gate, inviting them to slow down, breathe, and enter a world of serenity, much like stepping from a bustling Japanese street into a shrine's stillness. My intent was clear: to create a space where peace enveloped each soul, lifting them with love and healing.

Throughout this time, I witnessed firsthand how the principles we practiced made a real difference—students later shared stories of sensing danger early, avoiding confrontation, and, in some cases, surviving serious threats because of the awareness and grounding they cultivated in training. People often ask if I have ever used Aikido in a "real" situation. I tell them I use it every day—not in combat, but in awareness, presence, and prevention. True self-defense begins long before conflict arises—with prevention, awareness, and trusting the wisdom of one's own gut. If a situation escalates to physical technique, it often means earlier opportunities for resolution were missed. Ultimately, the deepest realization came later, as I share in *Releasing Fear*: that true power arises when we recognize there is no separate self to defend.

Over the years, I came to see that Aikido's depth reaches far beyond technique. It is not merely a set of movements or a philosophy held in the mind—it is an embodiment of peace. Embodiment takes root on the mat, but its true flowering happens in daily life. Every moment has become a practice of blending rather than resisting, softening rather than hardening, meeting each arising circumstance with openness. This is the Way of Harmony—not only in training halls, but in every step, every breath, every encounter. Aikido has become not just something I do; it is something I am becoming.

One afternoon, training at full intensity with an advanced student, we practiced with the jō—a four-foot wooden staff, an Aikido weapon shaped by Morihei Ueshiba to teach blending and neutralizing attacks through circular spirals. His strikes grew harder, fiercer, while I softened, flowing with each movement. Then—snap. My consciousness parted, awareness stretching outward in 360 degrees and beyond. I felt his intent, his breath, the dojo's pulse—then further: a bird sipping from a stream outside, sunlight bursting through new green leaves, shadows dancing in patterns across the foliage. Time slowed, stretched; I was everything and nothing, a unity I would later touch again in meditation, held in radiant stillness.

That moment lingered. Another afternoon, a student's swift strike met me, and I moved without thought—my body open, my spirit still. Time softened, and I sensed that same presence moving through me, flowing through my hands, joining us in quiet harmony.

"How did you know?" he asked, bowing, eyes wide. I didn't know. I had simply surrendered into the flow.

In 2009, I wandered Japan's sacred shrines—Tokyo, Nara, Shingu—practicing with an eighty-year-old sensei whose movements flowed like water over stone. At a mountain temple, I sat beneath ancient cedars. The scent of pine hung thick in the air, the world hushed by reverence. Stillness settled, and I saw with clarity: Aikido was love embodied—a path not of resisting, but of reconciling, meeting each soul where they stood, redirecting force into peace. I had touched this understanding as a child, in quiet closets and music's silence, and here, through the spiraling blend of a movement, it found me anew. This art, begun at eighteen and now practiced at sixty-two, has softened my defenses, turning fear into trust, revealing a calm others call "a secret," an inner energy, a stillness within.

PERHAPS YOU'VE FELT this too—that sacred moment when resistance melts, and you find yourself moving in perfect flow, when sensitivity no longer feels like a burden but reveals itself as a gift. For me, Aikido became a living prayer, harmonizing spirit and body—much like my work with fascia and the spirit world—revealing what endures: a current of Love flowing through us, uniting all things, the only eternal thread.

That night in Japan, beneath a starlit sky that mirrored the infinite within, I whispered words of gratitude—to the mat, the masters, and the long arc of years between my first fall and this quiet moment of clarity. They taught me that peace arises not from force or control, but from surrender: a sacred letting go that aligns us with Love, a quiet wisdom that anchors me still.

Even now, each time I step onto the mat—both as student and sensei—I return to that quiet wisdom: the breath that centers, the bow that humbles, and the beauty of Love flowing through all things.

INVITATION TO PAUSE

- How might approaching conflict or challenge as an opportunity to blend rather than clash change your relationships and daily interactions?
- Consider a practice or discipline that has taught you something deeper than its surface techniques. How has embodying that practice transformed not just what you do, but who you are becoming?
- Reflect on moments when you've experienced expanded awareness—times when your consciousness seemed to stretch beyond ordinary boundaries. What did those experiences reveal about the nature of connection and presence?
- What would it mean to live each day as a practice of embodying peace—not just in formal settings, but in every breath, every step, every encounter?

THREAD OF RESISTANCE

"Victory over another fades. Victory over the self endures."

In 1980, the political tensions surrounding the Olympic Games—USA versus Soviet Union—left me disheartened. With my kayaking dreams dashed, I enlisted in the Air Force—a spontaneous leap. The recruiter promised a position in the medical field—an area that interested me—along with the opportunity to travel. My father's parting words still echo in my memory: "You're too damn independent to go into the Air Force." In defiance, I signed up the next day. His prediction proved more accurate than I realized.

I had yet to see how fiercely the lifelong battle between obedience and independence would be tested. Basic training at Lackland Air Force Base presented challenges I hadn't fully anticipated. The physical demands didn't trouble me; I could handle the exertion as an athlete used to intense training. The screaming TIs, though, were especially daunting for an introvert with a contemplative nature. The constant barrage of noise and aggression was intense by design—intended to break down individual identity regardless of one's character.

During basic training, we faced relentless inspections—from perfectly made beds with military corners to meticulously arranged clothing drawers where items had to be folded, aligned, and stacked with precision. After being reprimanded once for improper organization of my clothing drawer, I devised a solution—a creative rebellion. I carefully ironed all my T-shirts, underwear, and socks, arranged them with exact measurements—then left them untouched. The clothes became display pieces, perfect for inspection. Meanwhile, I wore only the clothes I kept in my laundry bag at the foot of my bed, cleaning them regularly but never disturbing my immaculate clothing drawer arrangement. I even received a rare compliment from a TI: "Best drawer I've seen," a small victory in a system designed to find fault.

The military's approach was methodical: break you down completely, then rebuild you as a soldier. They aimed to erase individual identity in favor of collective obedience. We drilled endlessly, learning to march in formation, to move and respond as one unified body. My body complied, but something in my spirit refused to yield.

The first act of defiance emerged during marching drills. There was a particular cadence I refused to sing:

"N-U-K-E, N-U-K-E,

Nuke 'em, Nuke 'em,

Kill, Kill, Kill!"

We were instructed to stomp hard on our right foot with each "Kill," emphasizing our commitment to destruction. Each time it came up, my voice fell silent while those around me shouted with programmed enthusiasm. It was a small resistance, barely noticeable, but eventually, someone noticed.

Summoned to the commander's office, I stood at attention as he unleashed a torrent of rage about duty, obedience, and my failure to embrace the warrior ethos. I remained silent until he demanded an explanation.

"I didn't join to 'kill, kill, kill,' sir," I said simply. "I joined to defend and serve in the medical field. I don't want to nuke anyone."

His face reddened. For a moment, I thought my military stint might end before it began. But after a long, uneasy silence, he granted me permission to refrain from that particular cadence—warning that any further resistance would not be tolerated.

Rather than relief, this small victory sparked a deeper defiance within me. This wasn't mere stubbornness or rebellion for its own sake. It was a refusal to betray my core values, even under intense pressure to conform. The tension between external expectations and inner truth was familiar territory, echoing earlier struggles with my father. Over time, I came to understand that true surrender isn't blind obedience—it is allegiance to one's deepest truth. In moments when my back was against the wall and threats loomed largest, something within me didn't cower—it ignited. This pattern, this quiet resistance to force, would later shape my approach to Aikido, where meeting force with force only creates more conflict. But at the time, that knowing had not yet taken root.

My duties expanded to include serving as road guard during marches, running ahead to block traffic while the formation passed. During one march, my hat—known as "cover" in military parlance—slipped forward, nearly obscuring my vision. I had to tilt my head back just to see. Military protocol forbade adjusting one's uniform without permission, so I remained still, partially blinded, faithfully following the last order given.

Unbeknownst to me, a TI approached from behind. His hand reached for my hat, and my body reacted instinctively—my fist flew up in his face, nearly striking him. I immediately snapped back to attention, bracing for the inevitable explosion of rage.

Instead, he stared at me with an inscrutable expression, then simply said, "Fix your damn cover," before walking away. In that moment, I sensed a reluctant respect—perhaps an unspoken recognition of the very spirit they were trying to both break and harness.

Upon graduating from basic training, I received my first shock of military reality: despite the recruiter's promises, I would not be entering the medical field. Instead, I was assigned to Lowry Air Force Base in Colorado for technical training as an Aircraft Armament Systems Specialist.

The irony wasn't lost on me—the recruit who had refused to chant about killing would now be trained to load bombs and maintain weapons systems. This wasn't about pacifism; I wasn't opposed to all forms of military service. But I found there was something deeply incongruent between my personal values and being immersed in systems designed solely for destruction.

During technical school at Lowry Air Force Base, I discovered the art of strategic evasion. My resistance evolved, revealing more creative opportunities as I learned to navigate the system.

One particularly frigid day followed one of the biggest snowstorms in the city's history. More than three feet of snow had fallen, and we were summoned for a surprise inspection in the quad. The purpose? To catch those of us wearing non-regulation warm socks instead of the standard-issue black ones that offered little protection against the Colorado winter.

As we stood freezing in formation, the squad leader announced, "Anyone with a medical appointment is excused." Without hesitation, I marched toward the medical unit, despite having no appointment. My warm socks and I escaped detection, another small triumph of individual thinking in a system that demanded conformity.

After attending technical school, I was assigned to the 355th Equipment Maintenance Squadron at Davis-Monthan Air Force Base in Tucson, Arizona. In the relentless desert heat, the scent of jet fuel and metal hung in the air as I walked each morning to the maintenance hangar.

My days were filled with learning about the A-10 Thunderbolt II—nicknamed the "Warthog." This air-to-ground fighter was renowned for its devastating 30mm Gatling gun mounted in the nose, designed to destroy tanks and ground targets. I studied bomb racks, missile launchers, and gun systems—how to mount, load, and maintain them to ensure they could effectively deliver destruction when called upon.

Each day pushed me further from my original intention, delving deeper into a system I increasingly questioned. Beyond the weaponry, the economic priorities troubled me—millions poured into machines while need lingered elsewhere. The contradiction was stark—communities across America struggling for basic resources while this massive war machine consumed limitless funding.

Perhaps most disturbing was the institutional waste I witnessed. One day, we received orders to throw away brand-new supplies—bolts, giant rolls of duct tape, and other still-packaged materials—simply to deplete the budget so we could qualify for the same funding level the following year. As I tossed these valuable resources, I wondered: was I defending my country—or participating in an assault on common sense and fiscal responsibility? The question lingered, unanswered, as I continued my duties.

My father's words echoed: "You're too damn independent." He had seen what I couldn't—that my nature would inevitably clash with the military's demand for unquestioning obedience.

The warrior spirit within me wasn't the problem; many exceptional soldiers possess it. It was my resistance to wielding that spirit in service of destruction instead of protection that created the fundamental conflict.

This experience became a crucible, forcing me to confront the disconnect between my inner truth and my outward commitments. When I eventually received an honorable discharge, the relief was profound—like setting down a weight I hadn't fully realized I'd been carrying. I stepped back into civilian life with quiet gratitude—and a deep hunger to live in alignment with my truest values. That thread of resistance had not been a weakness. It was a compass. And it would guide me forward—toward peace, presence, and the art of blending with life without betraying myself.

INVITATION TO PAUSE

- Consider times when you've felt caught between external expectations and your inner truth. How did you navigate that tension, and what did those experiences teach you about authentic living?
- Reflect on moments when your resistance to something revealed deeper values you weren't fully aware you held. What did that resistance illuminate about who you truly are?
- Where in your life might you be participating in systems that conflict with your core values? What would it take to realign your actions with your deepest convictions?
- How do you distinguish between healthy resistance that protects your integrity and stubborn defiance that serves no greater purpose?

PART III

Surrender's Path

PREFACE TO PART III

Surrender became my greatest teacher—not as defeat or resignation, but as an opening to grace. Through years of seeking, I discovered that true power emerges not from control or force, but from alignment with a deeper flow. This path unfolded in unexpected ways—from loading bombs in the Air Force to walking the silent halls of monasteries; from facing danger on a dark French road to healing through the crystalline web of fascia; from taming a wolf to tending the wildness within.

Each experience reveals different facets of the same truth: when I released struggle and flowed with life rather than against it, something profound emerged—a strength beyond my limited self, a quiet presence that carried me through even the most challenging of circumstances. These stories trace my journey from outward striving to inner stillness, from seeking peace in the world to embodying it from within.

What began as a quest for meaning gradually transformed into a life of presence—touching spirit through many forms, guiding others toward wholeness, and resting more fully in the Love that holds us all. I share these experiences not as a blueprint to follow, but as reflections of a universal invitation that calls to each of us in unique ways. Perhaps in these stories, you'll recognize your own moments of surrender—those times when letting go opened you to something greater than anything effort alone could achieve.

THE FLYING NUN

"True freedom is found not in leaving the world behind,
but in carrying stillness within wherever you go."

After leaving military service, I began a journey that would unfold over more than a decade—exploring a different kind of service through religious life, seeking my place among various communities and listening for where Spirit might call me next. This path first led to South Dakota, where I lived and worked with a Benedictine community serving the Sioux Nation on the Indian Reservation. I later spent the summer in Los Angeles with the Dominican School Sisters, where I helped teach English and math to underprivileged children. I remember one evening during community hour, the room humming with sisters chatting, some watching the news, others reading papers. An older sister taught me to knit, her hands guiding mine as needles clicked. I beamed at my progress. She stood, praised me—then, with a grin, began slowly unraveling it back to a single flaw.

I laughed, her slow undoing a playful lesson, and the room erupted in shared joy—a moment of pure grace in community. I came to cherish communal life—its shared vision and sisterhood. Within each community, I found a life where prayer and service were woven together, a path I glimpsed in shared silence and the song of different spiritual traditions.

With modest savings and a one-way ticket, I landed in eastern England at an ancient manor, a Tudor haven where Catholic sisters hosted interfaith gatherings at their conference center. During my year there, I tended its chapel and gardens, my hands brushing stones first laid in 1525. Their cool, weathered surfaces had borne witness to centuries of devotion and prayer. When assigned to clean the floors, one sister and I laughed about 'scrubbing rocks,' finding grace in how perspective could transform any task—into burden or blessing. In the quiet halls, I began to recognize each sister by the sound of her steps, each tread a distinct echo. I was deeply drawn to this life where every task became prayer.

It was in that weathered library that I first discovered Thomas Merton's *The Seven Storey Mountain*, a work that awakened a deep longing in me for a life of solitude and prayer. Later, I encountered his vivid descriptions of Christ in the Desert Monastery—the most remote monastery in the United States—a stone refuge cradled by the red-rock mountains of New Mexico. His reflections deepened my resolve: to immerse myself more fully in silence and solitude.

I began writing letters to the brothers, asking if I might come for an extended stay. As this was an unusual request, our correspondence unfolded slowly, across many months. After celebrating my twenty-first birthday with the sisters, I left the convent in England and embarked on a twelve-week pilgrimage through Europe. I spent four weeks at the Taizé Community in France, then joined thousands of young people gathered for a week of prayer and dialogue on world peace, at Notre Dame Cathedral in Paris. With my backpack over my shoulder, I continued my journey to Rome, for the closing of the Holy Year where I was among a group of young people who met Pope John Paul II, Mother Teresa, and Brother Roger of Taizé—encounters that stirred a quiet recognition of the path I was being called to. I ended my pilgrimage in Assisi, carrying with me a quiet certainty that solitude and prayer were no longer longings, but home.

At last, I received a letter from the brothers, granting me permission to stay at the desert monastery for an initial three months—an uncommon welcome in a place where guests were usually received only for short stays.

REACHING the monastery was a pilgrimage in itself—not just distant, but deliberately so. I was picked up by two of the brothers from the community: Brother André, the guest master, and Brother Xavier, whose long white beard and twinkling blue eyes gave him the look of a desert-born Santa Claus. We rode together in an old donated pickup truck, bumping along the narrow dirt road that wound through the red rock canyons for miles. The farther we traveled, the quieter everything became. Red-rock cliffs rose around us, the river weaving beside us like a silent companion. In those days, the road was often washed out—rutted, rough, and slow. No signs. No guardrails. No way to rush. The brothers knew every turn by heart, navigating with a calm ease that invited stillness. I sat quietly, the outside world falling further behind with every mile. By the time we reached the adobe walls of the monastery, I felt I had crossed more than rugged terrain—I had crossed a threshold into silence, into something that would begin to shape me from within. The isolation was complete and intentional, making the monastery one of the most remote in the country.

Brother Xavier's gentle presence would stay with me in ways I didn't expect. During Easter week, a young family visited the monastery for the liturgy, their little boy no more than five. As everyone gathered quietly in the chapel, the boy stared intently at Brother Xavier. Then suddenly he blurted out, "I want a truck for Christmas!" The entire chapel burst into laughter—Brother Xavier most of all. In a place steeped in silence, that child's innocent delight became a moment of pure joy, revealing the warmth that lived beneath the stillness.

This visit confirmed my calling to the contemplative life. After three months, I returned to complete my university studies in Theology and Philosophy, carrying the desert's stillness within me. This academic journey stirred my mind with questions rather than certainties. Upon graduating, the brothers welcomed me back—this time to live in a hermitage at the edge of the monastery grounds for almost a full year. What claim could I hold? A wanderer with empty hands. Yet they welcomed me—a solitary seeker among a sparse brotherhood, living by oil lamps and the warmth of wood stoves, where silence cloaked all doings, a stillness apart from the world's clamor.

Unlike the Benedictine communities tending the poor or Dominican sisters teaching—communities alive with outward care—this cloistered life turned inward, its heart beating in prayer and quiet labor. Their days flowed in sacred rounds—eight prayer gatherings from pre-dawn to the final chant at night, meals and work done in reverent silence.

I folded laundry—towers of linens rising like offerings, each fold a prayer—my fingers tracing the cadence of Gregorian chant, songs that enfolded my soul. It was here that prayer revealed itself not as an isolated act, but as a continuous presence—each breath, each movement, each moment, an opportunity to dwell in sacred awareness.

Winter draped the desert in snow, and I trudged from hermitage to chapel, drifts high as my waist, the cold a sharp embrace. This was one of the most remote monasteries in the United States—no electricity, no telephone, the nearest connection to the outside world was a two-hour drive along rugged dirt roads. Red-rock mountains loomed, their ancient faces catching the dawn's first light, the scent of wet sage rose after summer rain, cloudscapes blazing with color, and the eagle's cry pierced the quiet—yet the silence sang, a rhythm as steady as my own pulse, vast as the earth's hidden heart. At first, it roared—grief's echoes, shadows past—but I lingered, yielding to its hold. Each breath softened into presence, a prayer not bound to form but alive in the stillness. A simple verse hung in my hermitage—*"Be still and know that I am God. Be still and know. Be still. Be."*—its cadence became a living chant, an invitation to dwell in the eternal now.

This seeking carried me through more than thirteen years, with convents and cloisters becoming my spiritual home. After the monastery, my path led me to Milwaukee, where I lived and worked with a Franciscan community for over four years, hands outstretched to the poor and homeless; served as a youth minister for the archdiocese; and worked nights as a counselor at both a homeless shelter and a long-term shelter for battered women. I remember at St. Ben's soup kitchen, after serving over 400 meals, I was wiping down tables—one man lingered, cherishing each bite. He looked up with deep eyes, and I felt the grace between us: we each served the other, our roles unfolding into Love's sacred dance. His simple grace, etched in those eyes, stays with me still, a quiet blessing.

My family named me "the flying nun," a nod to my journey through various communities, offered with affectionate humor. Though I never took formal vows with any order, I held private vows—poverty and chastity, which I embraced—while traditional obedience remained elusive; my heart was vowed to God alone, to a life lived in service of Love. In the vast silence of that desert hermitage, with only red rocks and endless sky as witnesses, I met this call anew—not as weight, but as companion. Spirit's presence, constant since birth, flowed not through sound but through the quiet—a deep wellspring of communion.

The mystics who guided me—Ram Dass with his boundless now, Thich Nhat Hanh with his mindful breath, St. John of the Cross with his dark night, St. Francis with his simple love, and St. Teresa with her inner castle—seemed to dance together in that silent center. Their wisdom converging into a single truth: surrender is a path to freedom. The brothers watched my transformation—my hands grew steady, my eyes gentle. When I stepped forth, they nodded, wordless, as if I had touched what lies beyond seeking—a peace born of pure presence. In the refectory, the simple daily bread—dense, homemade, still warm—offered sustenance beyond mere calories. Each bite a meditation, the taste of wheat and yeast an earthly communion that nourished both body and spirit. Yet even now, many years later, I can close my eyes and find myself there—folding linens as ancient chants rise and fall, each movement a prayer, each breath a return to the formless center.

Eventually, the time came to step beyond the monastery's physical embrace. Standing at the threshold between two worlds—structured silence and the world's ceaseless movement—I felt a mixture of sadness and anticipation. I would soon be joining a Franciscan community of sisters, which brought its own excitement amid my discernment, though I deeply treasured the silence and sacred rhythm of monastic life.

During the first weeks away, the ordinary sounds of traffic and distant voices were overwhelming after a year of stillness broken only by wind through juniper and the brothers' chants. Yet I discovered that the silence had become portable—a presence carried within, accessible even in crowded streets or busy rooms, a sanctuary not of stone but shaped by breath and sacred attention.

Looking back now, I see that my years among religious communities were like the monastery bells—each in its own way calling me to presence, each summoning a deeper surrender. Those bells marked time not by minutes, but by invitation—to prayer, to service, to silence. Though I no longer live within those stone walls, I carry their rhythm within me. Each moment still arrives like a small bell ringing, inviting me to return to Love's center. What once appeared as wandering was, in truth, a pilgrimage inward—toward the heart of surrender.

The Flying Nun's path was not merely a journey between communities, but a gradual soaring toward freedom—my wings not stitched of habit cloth, but woven from the expanding awareness of presence. Through this unfolding, I came to understand that we serve best when we release even the idea of server and served. That prayer deepens as words fall away. And that surrender—once seen by my younger self as defeat—revealed itself as the very threshold into Love's embrace.

This remains the heart of the path I walked: the chapel of surrender is not built of stone, but formed in stillness. And I dwell there still—in Love's quiet embrace.

INVITATION TO PAUSE

- Consider the places, practices, or rhythms that invite you into sacred presence. How do these shape your daily experience?
- Reflect on accessing inner stillness even amid external chaos. What cultivates this capacity for presence wherever you go?
- Where in your life do you sense the invitation to move beyond seeking toward simply being?
- What would it mean to trust that you've already found what you've been looking for?
- How might approaching each moment as "a small bell ringing" transform your awareness of the sacred in ordinary life?

RELEASING FEAR

*"What is eternal needs no defense. Illusion fades,
but truth remains untouched by fear."*

At twenty-one, I wandered the French countryside, a young seeker trekking toward Taizé, a haven of chant and prayer that called to my soul. The day had stretched long, my backpack heavy with purpose, when dusk began to cloak the rolling hills. Five miles remained when a car slowed beside me, a man leaning out with a kind voice and an offer of a ride. Grateful, I accepted, sliding my pack into the back, trusting the moment's grace. But, as we drove, he veered from the main road, turning down a dirt path shrouded by trees. Darkness fell, and with it, a chilling clarity: I was in danger.

Fear surged through me like a current, electric and wild and undeniable. My body shook—knees knocking, hands trembling—as my nervous system braced for a fight I could not yet define. The man's intent hung heavy in the air, unspoken but unmistakable, as the car wound deeper into isolation. I saw the scene unfold before me: a struggle, a blade, a final breath—his or mine. In that moment, I prayed to the Mother of Jesus, a woman who would understand such peril, a mother whose fierce protection steadied me: *"If this begins, only one of us will walk away from here."* There would be no middle ground. And in that instant, I released all attachment to my life—all fear of death—and a deep, unwavering calm washed over me.

The shaking ceased, replaced by a stillness I had glimpsed in near-death's embrace—a calm alight with fierce presence. The most dangerous person in the world is the one who has nothing to lose—I released everything, even my life. You cannot take a life already surrendered; there was no life left to claim but his. What rose in me was not passive, but potent, akin to a warrior's clarity before battle, born of letting go. A strange compassion stirred for this man I would kill if needed—simple, unclouded by anger or fear, like stepping down a staircase, the next obvious step. In that stillness, I saw beyond our roles—potential victim, looming threat—and recognized us as souls, each playing our part in this human drama, tethered by an inevitable thread.

From that radiant depth, I turned to him, lifted my hand, and pointed directly at his face. The crucifix ring on my left hand marked a private vow—a quiet, sacred promise between my heart and God to live a life of love and service. In that moment, it became more than a symbol; it became a blade of light, a line drawn in spirit, reminding me who I was. I spoke with direct command: "You will restart this car now. You will take me to the nearest town. And tomorrow morning, you will return and take me where you should have." His face drained of color, as if staring steadily into death itself. The roles reversed—he now trembled, overtaken by fear. No other choice remained. As if in a trance, he restarted the engine and obeyed my command.

He drove me to a small town and left me at a hotel. The next morning, he returned, ashen but compliant, and completed the journey to Taizé. As I stepped from the car, he muttered, "Be careful out there—it's a dangerous world." I reached into my pack, pulled out a Franciscan cross, and pressed it into his hand. "I will see you again someday," I said, with quiet certainty, sensing that our paths would cross again beyond this life. He drove off, a teacher unwitting, his lesson now etched in me: the most powerful person in the world is the one who has nothing to lose.

In the days that followed at Taizé, I moved through chants and silence like someone newly born. The peace I had touched in that car didn't fade—it deepened. I realized I had been given a gift: not just survival, but a glimpse into the strength that comes when all fear falls away. That moment continued to shape my path, reminding me again and again that true protection arises not from walls or weapons, but from alignment with the Presence of Love within.

That encounter revealed a visceral truth: power arises not from force, but from alignment with the universe's flow. By releasing all, I tapped a strength transcending my small self—a wellspring forged across lifetimes of facing fear and death. In that stillness, I became the universe, not merely a part of it. Every challenge, no matter how daunting, holds a gift: the chance to expand, to remember our infinite and unshakable essence.

Perhaps you have brushed this edge too—a moment when fear dissolved into freedom, unveiling your limitless essence. For me, this encounter wove Aikido's lessons, near-death's whispers, and love's fierce power into one. Beneath that French sky, I found not just survival, but a stillness that transforms fear into freedom—a peace I share with you now.

INVITATION TO PAUSE

- Consider a time when you felt truly threatened or endangered. How did you respond, and what did that experience reveal about your inner strength?
- Reflect on moments when releasing attachment—to outcomes, safety, or even life itself—paradoxically gave you more power. What did that teach you about the nature of true freedom?

- Where in your life might you be operating from fear rather than from the deep stillness that comes with complete surrender? How might your approach shift if you truly had nothing to lose?
- Think about someone who has been a difficult teacher in your life. Can you recognize the unexpected gifts that emerged from that challenging encounter?
- What would it mean to trust that your deepest protection comes not from external defenses, but from alignment with Love's presence within you?
- Let your breath return you to that still point—
- the place within you that cannot be taken.

THE WOLF'S ROAD

"The heart's awakening is the only revolution
that will bring lasting peace."

In my late twenties, I lived among religious communities passionate about social justice, my heart tethered to a cry for peace. I marched with a group protesting U.S. involvement in Central America, speaking out against death squads and the terror campaigns waging guerrilla wars. The air in Washington buzzed with determination as more than ten thousand of us gathered, our voices rising in unison and our signs gleaming in the sunlight. Our footsteps created a rhythm of resistance on pavement that had witnessed generations of protest. A friend, a religious sister, had lost her life in El Salvador amidst that turmoil—a calling I nearly followed, tempted to join her community. Yet my strong will, shaped by years of seeking, cautioned me: I might meet the same fate. Instead, I chose to march, protest, and stand firmly in nonviolent dissent.

Arrests were frequent. Once, I found myself locked in a cell no larger than a closet, three days consumed by noise, filth, and harsh lights that never dimmed. While small spaces held no fear for me, the jails were a cacophony—dirty, odorous, relentless. I asked myself, "How far am I willing to go for peace?" In one crowded holding cell, about thirty women sat together in tense silence when the door clanged open. A woman entered, her body coiled with rage, her eyes scanning for conflict. Her furious presence filled the already stifling air as she paced and muttered threats. While others recoiled, I observed her reaching for her neck, pain threading through her anger. After watching for a while, I cautiously approached her, offering to help ease her discomfort. Reluctance flashed across her face but then softened into acceptance as she allowed me to work on her tense muscles while she lay on the concrete floor. As my hands found the knots of her suffering, her breathing slowed, her face softened, and eventually, she drifted into sleep. Her transformation brought a gift of peace to everyone in that cell—a small healing that rippled outward in an unlikely place.

During another jail stay, I witnessed an elderly woman standing by a barred window, tears streaming down her weathered face as she peered through the grimy mesh screen. "I can't see anything anymore," she whispered, her voice cracking with despair. I stood beside her, feeling the weight of her words echoing beyond the literal. Gently, I suggested we step back from the window together, moving just a few feet away. As we retreated, the city skyline and the distant shimmer of a lake came into focus through the dirty screen. Her face brightened with surprise at the suddenly clear view. This moment stayed with me—a living parable illustrating that sometimes we need distance to gain clarity, and stepping back can reveal what pressing close obscures.

Archbishop Oscar Romero's life—his strength and martyrdom in 1980—illuminated my path. His steady voice against violence echoed in my soul, urging me to stand for love amid chaos. Yet one protest changed everything. As police bound our wrists, a religious sister beside me resisted—twisting against the plastic restraints, her habit stark against the gray concrete, her eyes narrowed not in physical pain but in rage. We were there for peace and nonviolence, offering no fight—but her struggle was not with them. I looked into her eyes, ablaze with inner conflict, and a question pierced me: "What are you really fighting? Where does your anger stem from?" In that moment, I saw my own rage —deep-seated and raw, rooted not in Central America's wounds, but in scars buried within my own heart. I realized that the troubles of the world mirrored a collective ache—one that could only be healed from the inside out, not the outside in.

That realization turned me homeward. Like the woman at the jail window, I needed to step back to see clearly. Weeks later, I traded my motorcycle—my only means of transport—for a wolf hybrid pup named Tundra, a silver-gray-black companion with deep, dark brown eyes that seemed to peer directly into my soul's wild edge. He was three-quarters Timber Wolf and one-quarter Shepherd, embodying both wildness and loyalty. When I first picked him up, the previous owner offered one clear warning: "He will be a powerful animal. One day he will challenge you. You must be the alpha. If you let him win that challenge, you'll lose him—he'll be uncontrollable."

I had always been afraid of dogs. When I was just five, I had been attacked by a loose dog that nearly took my eye, leaving vivid memories of teeth lunging toward my face. I decided to confront this fear by choosing the largest, strongest dog I could find. The irony wasn't lost on me—selecting a wolf to overcome my fear of dogs was akin to diving into the ocean to conquer a fear of water. Yet something in his dark gaze called to a wilder part of me, one that understood survival, boundaries, strength, and surrender.

As he grew, Tundra's paws matched the size of my palm, his body reaching 120 pounds of muscle and intelligence. True to the warning, he did challenge me one day—teeth bared, power surging through his massive frame. In that moment, I faced a crossroads: yield and lose our bond, or meet his challenge with equal strength. Not wanting to lose him, I held him on his back, my fist at his throat—a primal language he understood. He never challenged me again.

Tundra became my teacher in the subtle language of the wolf—a language of respect, boundaries, and permission. Each evening, he would lay his head on my chest, a gesture of trust and connection, before taking his place as a sentinel at my bedroom door. For fourteen years, he walked beside me on my inward journey, his presence a constant reminder of the balance between wildness and domestication, strength and tenderness. Some angels have wings, and some have fur—guardians appearing in the forms we need most.

With my belongings packed in a rented van and Tundra by my side, we ventured across the country to my home state—the highway unspooling beneath us like a meditative path, each mile a prayer of return.

I let go of the vision of joining a religious community and chose instead to mend my bond with my father and return to university. I completed master's degrees in Exercise Physiology/Kinesiology and Family Counseling, forging my path toward somatic healing—before such programs formally existed. However, my journey with my father faltered—his walls unyielding, and mine too. I realized I needed to go deeper—beyond him—to work within the generational patterns that only I could begin to shift from within. I came to see that love flows not from the outside in, but from the inside out. Before I could truly receive love, I had to unravel the inherited beliefs and layered defenses that had taken root within me.

As Mahatma Gandhi said, "Be the change you wish to see in the world." For me, that change began with healing my inner landscape—before I could hope to transform anything beyond myself. A decade of cloisters and chants had gently masked a quiet bypass: a spiritual devotion that softly veiled wounds I had not yet faced. What followed was over ten years of inner excavation. Psychotherapy became not confession but discovery—an uncovering, layer by layer, of the parts of me I had once deemed unlovable. I realized that I could not give what I did not yet hold within. If I wished to guide others toward wholeness—if I longed for peace not just in the world, but within—I had to walk the path fully, to heal the web at its source, and to begin within.

What I once offered that angry woman in the cell—tending to pain with gentle hands—I now extended inward, to myself. Love's deepest well, I discovered, springs not from silence alone, but from facing the places we most fear to touch.

The mystics who had guided me—Ram Dass with his boundless now, Thich Nhat Hanh with his mindful breath, St. John of the Cross with his dark night—reminded me that surrender is not defeat but the doorway to grace. Like wolves that must first map their territory before roaming free, I came to understand that peace begins with making peace within.

Tundra had been teaching me this all along—how to navigate the edge between wildness and loyalty, power and presence. My years of protests and prayers had circled this truth. Now I understood: the roads of outer justice and inner healing are not separate trails, but a single path.

I believe that every moment, every encounter, is an invitation to expand our capacity to love—or to retreat. So now I often ask myself, especially in difficult moments: "Can I love even this?" By tending to the wounded places within, I help mend the wider web of the world.

This is the paradox of surrender: in releasing the battle within, we become more powerful agents of healing without. That quiet wisdom walks beside me—as faithful a companion as Tundra once was—guiding me still through landscapes both wild and sacred.

INVITATION TO PAUSE

- Consider your own relationship with anger and activism. How do you distinguish between righteous action that serves healing and reactive behavior that perpetuates conflict?
- Reflect on times when you've needed to step back to gain clarity, like the woman at the jail window. What became

visible when you created distance from a situation you'd been pressing too close to?

- Where in your life might you be fighting external battles that are actually reflections of inner conflicts needing attention and healing?
- Think about the "wolves" in your life—the challenging relationships or circumstances that have taught you about boundaries, respect, and authentic power. What have these difficult teachers shown you?
- How might approaching each moment as "an invitation to expand your capacity to love—or to retreat" transform your daily interactions and responses to conflict?

SILENT SURRENDER

"Silence is not empty—it holds the presence of all that is."

Every life unfolds through breath. As a child, I first became aware of the unfolding within the stillness between breaths, words, and notes, where awareness quietly arose. In my late forties, an intensive meditation retreat called to me—ten days of immersion, nearly eleven hours of daily sitting meditation, an invitation to dwell solely in the awareness of breath.

This ancient practice, called Vipassana—meaning "to see things as they really are"—offered a direct invitation into awareness, a way of simply noticing what is rather than striving for insight. With meals prepared and responsibilities set aside, only the silent call to sit remained.

In the predawn darkness, a bell sounded at 4 AM, its resonance lingering in the chill air—a gentle summons not to labor but to rest in utter stillness. I rose from sleep, my cushion a quiet refuge, my body softening into the rhythm of the practice. From the early morning awakening to the 9:30 PM final meditation, the day unfolded in long arcs of silence—seventeen hours shaped by breath, stillness, and simplicity. Breakfast arrived at 6:30—oatmeal, dates, a humble apple—with only fruit and tea at five to carry us through the evening. Noble Silence held us—no words, no gestures, no reading or writing. Yet this was not absence but a deliberate tending of inner quiet, unmarred by devices or distraction. Just the steady presence of breath and being.

The first days centered on a gentle focus of observing the breath. As I walked the path to the hall, guided by starlight piercing the predawn darkness, I focused on my breath, breathing in and breathing out—as if meeting it anew. The hall filled with about a hundred practitioners, each finding their place in the dim light, men and women seated apart yet joined in silent purpose. At the front sat our teacher, his still presence a wordless invitation, guiding us deeper into our own silence. I entered the practice not as one seeking mastery but as a student with an empty cup, receptive to whatever might arise within the silence. The wooden floor beneath my cushion greeted me like an old friend, its solid presence supporting stillness.

On the fourth day, we transitioned to Vipassana itself—the systematic scanning of bodily sensations with equanimity—and I marveled at the elegant simplicity of this ancient technique. "Start at the crown of the head," came the teacher's gentle instruction, "and move methodically downward, part by part, observing each sensation without reaction." By this time, my body ached from the hours of sitting; the challenge was not to resist but to observe. This witnessing state brought a sense of recognition—meeting pain without resistance, acknowledging pleasure without attachment. Equanimity, a faithful companion through quiet practice, deepened into something more profound—each bodily sensation revealing itself as merely a passing visitor, arising, lingering briefly, then dissolving, each one a quiet teaching in impermanence.

This practice of observing—what Ram Dass beautifully described as "no pushing or pulling"—became a profound healing gift years later. After a neck injury in 2019, I faced tremendous pain that triggered the natural tendency to tighten against it, fearing it would never end—resistance that only intensified the suffering. When a doctor delivered the stern warning that even one more bump could leave me quadriplegic, fear threatened to overwhelm me. In that dark moment, the Vipassana training emerged like a lighthouse, offering a narrow path through the storm. By gently observing the pain without pushing it away or clinging to it, I discovered I could witness its changing nature—how even the most intense sensations rose, shifted, and eventually transformed. This simple truth—that nothing stays the same—became more than an abstract understanding. It became my lived refuge, a quiet shelter within my own awareness where, even amid physical distress, I could find moments of peace by simply witnessing rather than struggling against what is.

As the days of meditation unfolded, the outer world receded while inner awareness expanded. Thoughts continued to surface as they always do. I practiced meeting their presence without inviting them to stay for tea, simply remaining a gentle witness to their coming and going. Each hour deepened this capacity to observe without entanglement. Then, in the crystalline silence of day seven, something shifted.

In the hall's deep silence, a man coughed across the room—an ordinary sound piercing the quiet. The cough rippled through my awareness like a pebble skipping across still water, vibrations felt with startling vividness. Curious, I thought, 'Do that again.' As if in answer, he coughed once more, and the sensation danced across my perception, waves spreading outward through my body and beyond, rippling through everything in their path.

Then, with a sudden unveiling, reality shifted—the room and even my own form dissolving into countless particles of light. These luminous points flowed like a vast sea of consciousness, carrying my awareness beyond all boundaries. Where solid bodies and walls had stood only moments before, I now perceived only fluid vibration, pulsing and flowing. No boundaries remained—I was everyone and everything, the meditators, the floor, the air, all one ceaseless flow of consciousness.

Resting in this boundless expanse, I was simultaneously everything and nothing, all edges and separations dissolving, awareness clear and limitless. I perceived the unity beneath all form—a vast ocean of consciousness where distinctions between self and other faded away. Then, almost playfully, I discovered that by shifting my focus to a single point, form would return instantly—solidity taking shape wherever I directed my attention. Fascinated, I explored this dance, watching energy gather and disperse at will. I experienced reality not as something fixed but as a dynamic interplay of awareness and vibration—not as an abstract concept but as a lived experience, a play of consciousness breathing in and breathing out, forming and returning to formlessness.

The final days of the retreat deepened the experience—each sitting becoming a graceful return to centeredness, breath flowing like a quiet tide, sensations drifting like whispers on the wind. The heightened awareness remained, though in a more subtle way, infusing each moment with clarity as I continued breathing in and breathing out.

On day ten, silence lifted, and voices suddenly filled the air as everyone embraced the chance to speak after days of quiet. A woman nearby, her gaze gentle and curious, approached me. "You seemed so still throughout the retreat," she said, "as if you weren't even there." I smiled, uncertain how to respond. After a pause, I said quietly, 'Maybe sometimes I wasn't there,' and I laughed.

The world of sound returned like a wave—conversations flowing, laughter rippling, the percussion of footsteps. After ten days of silence, even ordinary noises arrived with extraordinary presence—the scrape of chairs, the rustle of clothing, the wind's gentle breath against my skin. I moved with unhurried attention through this changing landscape, the silence no longer external but internalized—a bell whose resonance now rang from within, beneath and between each new sound.

Meditation for me is a practice of presence all hours of the day—not just sitting meditation but an awareness practice woven into daily life. This opportunity of Vipassana offered me depth in the art of surrender, not as retreat but as embrace—an allowing of flow in stillness, not just in sitting but as a way of being in every moment—whether washing dishes, sweeping floors, or walking streets—soap suds, broom's sweep, earth beneath my feet, all doorways to the infinite. What began as a warrior's breath continues unfolding into a practice of presence, a golden current carrying me through every storm and quiet moment, whispering we are never apart from the love that holds us all.

INVITATION TO PAUSE

- Consider your own relationship with silence. Where do you find the deepest quiet, and what does that stillness reveal to you about the nature of awareness itself?
- Reflect on times when observing difficult sensations or emotions without pushing them away or pulling them closer has transformed your experience. What did you discover about the changing nature of all phenomena?
- Where in your life might you benefit from approaching experiences "as if meeting them anew," with the freshness of a beginner's mind?
- Think about moments when the boundaries between self and other seemed to dissolve—perhaps in nature, in love, in creative flow. What did those experiences teach you about the underlying unity of existence?
- How might carrying an internalized silence—"a bell whose resonance rings from within"—change the way you move through your daily activities and interactions?

THE LUMINOUS WEB

"The soul holds the infinite in a single breath."

A boy's legs twisted like young branches, brittle under a rare bone disease—doctors planned to break them at four years old, reset them with metal and time. His mother carried him into my office, her eyes pleading: "Can you do anything?" I knelt beside his tiny frame, hands hovering over the fragile web of his body, and said, "Let's see." Months later, his legs reshaped—soccer fields became his playground, surgery forgotten. His doctors marveled, "Whatever you are doing, keep doing it —it's working." I did not break bones; I listened to the luminous web within—a crystalline lattice whispering balance, relationship, and connection.

Years earlier, I stood at a crossroads in a university classroom, a master's in Physical Therapy in my sight. Though my teachers urged a path I could not walk—training us as administrators, supervising assistants, tethered to desks and paperwork. I thought, "If I wanted to sit behind a desk, I would have gone to business school." My gift lived in my hands; the decision to carve another path crystallized one day after a neuroanatomy class. I ventured a thought to my instructor: "Consciousness does not arise from the brain—it is flowing in and through us, it is the ground substance of the physical form—a holographic expression, vibrations slowed."

He stared, incredulous, as if I had two heads. "That is not science," he scoffed. I knew it was—science broader than his microscope would ever see. Shortly after this conversation, I switched to Exercise Physiology and Kinesiology, vowing to design my own path, creating a space where my hands could express what language could never fully capture. Alongside, I pursued a master's in Family Counseling, with a focus on Gestalt therapy, knowing that spirit, mind, and body weave as one.

While studying at the university, a serendipitous opportunity arose when the Kinesiology Department needed a martial arts instructor for both Aikido and self-defense classes. I suggested that my Aikido sensei apply for the position. He responded with a smile, "No, you teach." I hesitated at the thought but then accepted the direction, understanding that teaching could deepen my own practice. I was both student and teacher, learning as much from them as they learned from me. I taught for over a decade at the university, which eventually led to the founding of my own martial arts school, Shinzen Dojo, in 2002. I became the head teacher of the school and some years later, I was promoted to 5th-degree black belt in Aikido.

The dojo and my healing practice became complementary expressions of the same understanding—that balance comes from attuning to energy rather than opposing it. In Aikido, I guided students to feel the invisible connections between their center and their partner's movements, teaching that true power came not from force but from alignment with universal principles. This mirrored what I discovered in bodywork—where the body's intelligence responded not to analysis, but to relationship, attention, and presence. A skilled martial artist doesn't resist an attack, but blends and redirects. My hands learned the same: sensing resistance in tissue and moving with it—not against—so transformation could arise. In Aikido, I taught blending with movement rather than resisting it; in my bodywork practice, I guided the fascia back to its alignment with gravity. Both became laboratories for exploring the luminous web that connects us all.

That path led me to Dr. Ida Rolf's Structural Integration, a practice based in osteopathic medicine, an art I practiced for over thirty years until COVID unraveled that chapter and gently pointed me in new directions. Rolf, a biochemist with a Ph.D. from Columbia in 1920, saw the body as a seamless web, not a machine of parts. Her work, born in the 1940s from yoga and osteopathy, realigned fascia—connective tissue —with gravity's pull, freeing vitality.

Everything is relationship. Fascia, that crystalline matrix wrapping muscles, bones, and nerves, hums with a piezoelectric spark—like quartz in a radio, it channels energy, information, and spirit. Strip the body down to this web, and a three-dimensional form remains—a microcosm of the universe's vast lattice, an information highway attuned to consciousness's broadcast in light, sound, and frequency. Like a holographic projection of consciousness, each part reflects the whole—every cell, every gesture, every healing moment echoing the greater pattern of wholeness that lives both within and around us. But in truth, there is no within or without—only a seamless field of being. We are living light, like nodes within a luminous web of consciousness, receiving and projecting, tuned to an infinite field of information.

In practice, I sought these patterns. A knee injury was never just a knee—feet faltered, a pelvis tilted, a life fell out of rhythm. A UPS driver leaned drastically right, his knee and back aching from years half-in, half-out of his truck. My hands traced the web upward, easing the tilt— he stood straighter, pain fading. A boy's elbow, broken in soccer and pinned by doctors, stiffened; they said full range would never return. He hid it under his jacket at school, ashamed. I worked with him, marking pencil lines on my office wall each week—soon, his arm stretched free. Now, when I see him in town, a grown man, he waves with an outstretched arm.

Another child, unable to walk, was brought by his aunt after a three-hour drive. Doctors offered no answers; after one session, he stood—

weeks later, he walked; months later, he ran, his aunt's eyes brimming with joy as she witnessed each milestone. The body amazes when we speak its language, just as I learned with Tundra, my wolf.

The boy with the bone disease remains etched in my memory. His tiny femur shifted under my hands, the web responding as I coaxed balance—feet to pelvis, pelvis to spine. His mother wept when he ran; I felt the web hum, a relationship restored.

A woman came, posture meek, voice soft—her husband's blows had bent both body and spirit. Through our sessions, her spine aligned, her power rose—she filed for divorce, standing tall, saying no more.

I came to see that fascia is not mere tissue but a living network—piezo-electric, like crystal—singing with the frequency of spirit. It exists at the intersection of the physical and the ineffable: a bridge between body and the field of consciousness, expressed through lived experience. Dr. Robert Schleip confirms its crystalline properties—under pressure, it sparks electric signals, a silent language of connection. I explained this to clients using a sea sponge: porous yet whole, every thread linked, holding the body's story.

This was not fixing—it was listening. The web knows its harmony; my hands simply helped it return. A client asked, "How did you know his arm could move again?" I didn't—his body knew. Consciousness flows through this lattice, not from the brain, as I told my instructor. Rolf knew it—her 1977 book, *Rolfing*, calls the brain a tuner, not the source, echoing ancient wisdom and quantum glimpses.

I followed breath, softening tension with no expectation, and space arose—bodies spoke what minds could not. Everything connects—within us, beyond us. These were synchronicities—like the child's sudden run or the woman's stand—events connected not by strict cause-and-effect but by a deeper connection between human and the universe. In these moments, when you are in the flow, everything is connected—there is only One.

For thirty years, I walked this road—Old Town Healing & Wellness became my healing space, hands my tools, the web my guide—until COVID brought it to a close in 2020. Clients dwindled; touch became forbidden. I let go, not of the web, but of that form, sensing another synchronicity calling me forward. Tundra had taught me trust; now the web taught me release. Healing is relationship, ever-moving, like Rolf's vision, a dynamic dance with gravity's grace.

I did not invent this—I attuned to it, a node within a vast luminous web, receiving each person's unique path to healing. The mystics—Rolf, Ram Dass, Gestalt's wholeness—whispered through: we are not separate from the cosmos, but intricately woven into it. The web glows beyond flesh—luminous, alive—linking my hands to a child's legs, a woman's spine, a universe humming with intent.

This luminous web reveals perhaps the deepest lesson of surrender I've encountered—not a passive giving up, but an active attunement to something far greater than our individual will. In my healing practice, as in Aikido, true mastery came not from imposing my agenda but from attuning to the body's innate intelligence—and finding the courage to follow where it led. What appeared as miraculous healing was often simply the natural unfolding that occurs when we remove barriers of resistance and allow ourselves to align with the greater patterns to which we belong. This surrender requires both strength and humility—strength to remain present with what is, and humility to recognize that we are not separate from but utterly woven into the fabric of existence itself. Healing starts here, in this crystalline dance of relationship, where spirit and body sing as one—a harmony only the open heart can comprehend.

INVITATION TO PAUSE

- Consider moments when you've experienced your body's innate intelligence—times when healing or knowing came not from your mind but from a deeper wisdom within. What did those experiences teach you about the body as teacher?

- Reflect on your own relationship with control versus attunement. Where in your life might you be trying to impose your will rather than listening to the greater patterns seeking to unfold?
- Think about the "webs" in your own life—the invisible connections between your physical, emotional, and spiritual well-being. How do changes in one area ripple through the others?
- Where have you witnessed what might be called "miraculous" healing or transformation? What conditions allowed such natural unfolding to occur?
- How might approaching your daily life as "a crystalline dance of relationship" change the way you interact with your body, your environment, and the people around you?

THE HEART'S FAREWELL

"What we love does not fade;
love lives on in the shape of who we become."

In my late forties, life gifted me a mentor whose spirit danced with light and shadow—Jim, a Gestalt therapist, a teacher of teachers, a man whose laughter could lift a room and whose violin sang with a tenderness that pierced the heart. He held his trainings at Shinzen Dojo, my sacred space of peace, once a month—gatherings where psychotherapists came to unravel the soul's knots with creativity and care. I was among them, a student hungry for his wisdom, and over time, a friend blessed by his presence. Our sessions created a sacred space between us—a field where we connected beyond words, where presence itself became the healing force. As with others I would later work deeply with, our communion transcended conventional therapy—it was a shared practice of presence, a conscious attunement to what might arise in each unfolding moment.

Once a month, I drove three hours north to sit with him one-on-

one, his gentle eyes meeting mine across a space that held both stillness and storm. In these encounters, I learned the power of simply being present—how two souls could merge into the rhythm of breath and heartbeat, creating a timeless space of unconditional love.

Not long before he left this world, a shadow crept into my awareness—a familiar whisper of death's nearness, a sensation I had known since infancy's fragile crossings. So vivid was this feeling that I convinced myself it was my own departure drawing near. One day, about a month before Jim's passing, I was taking a walk, deeply attuned to this sense of death's presence. I happened to pass a funeral home and, following an inner urging, walked in to inquire about making funeral arrangements. The costs shocked me—thousands upon thousands of dollars for elaborate caskets and services. Seeking something more aligned with simplicity, I found a pine box coffin for five hundred dollars—a stark contrast to the ten-thousand-dollar options they had shown me. This simple wooden coffin arrived at my home, a quiet preparation for what I still believed was my own passing, as I moved forward trusting the thread of spirit that had always guided me.

During one session with Jim, that whisper grew louder. I sat across from him, the air thick with an unspoken weight, and felt myself slip between worlds—a place I had touched in chapel pews and operating rooms, a luminous stillness where boundaries dissolve. Words faltered, but a longing stirred within me, a need to bridge the distance I sensed was widening between us. I asked, "May I rest my head on your heart?" He nodded, his kindness unwavering, and in silence I leaned forward, pressing my ear to his chest.

His heartbeat pulsed beneath me, distant and sad, mirroring the ache in my own. I prayed for peace—for him, for me—holding that moment as a fragile thread of love. The rhythm felt like an echo of farewells I had known before—Papa's, my brother's, Cassie's—yet I could not bear to name it his. I convinced myself the coffin was mine, a shield against the truth my soul already grasped. When the session ended, I stepped outside to a small fountain near his office, its water dripping in slow, glistening drops. I stood perfectly still, lost in a daze, watching each bead catch the light—essences of something vast shimmering beyond, a quiet invitation to trust what I could not yet see. In that moment, I was "poised on the edge of forever, riding the edge of time," as I would later write—caught between worlds, sensing what was coming yet unable to fully grasp it. Forty-five minutes passed, time unspooling like a thread, before I climbed into my car for the three-hour drive home.

The journey blurred—my eyes traced the red taillights of a semi-truck ahead, then lifted to the moon's pale glow, then back again, seeking a rhythm to steady my shaking hands. When I reached my house, I sat in the car, the world shaking around me—or so I thought. Then I realized it was not an earthquake, but my own body quaking.

For three weeks, my body trembled in waves beyond my control—a physical manifestation of trauma releasing itself from my cells. I was caught in a liminal tide not unlike what Jill Bolte Taylor describes in her stroke's unraveling—a dissolution of self, a surrender to something greater. I stood for hours in the shower, watching water cascade over me, willing the tremors to cease, praying to find solid ground. My jaw would shake uncontrollably, my limbs vibrating with energy seeking release. Finally, understanding dawned—this shaking was not something to fight, but to allow, a wisdom born of surrender. I lay down on my treatment table in my office and surrendered to it. For over an hour, the trembling moved through me like tides—intensifying, subsiding, returning—gradually working something ancient out of my system, my birth trauma perhaps now entwined with present grief. In surrender came wisdom: the body knows how to heal itself, if we only grant it permission.

The night before Jim's passing, I spoke with him by phone. His voice, usually strong, wavered with a fragile edge, a knot I could not unwind. He apologized repeatedly—for what, I did not know—and I listened, my heart breaking with each word. I managed only the most essential truth in that moment: "I love you, Jim." Three words that carried everything I couldn't articulate—my gratitude, my concern, my recognition of all he had been to me. That night, I retreated to my dojo, playing the didgeridoo's deep hum, tears streaming as I prayed without understanding why. The sound wove a bridge to spirit, a plea for peace I could not voice, a knowing I could not escape.

The next morning, word came: Jim had leapt from a bridge, choosing to end his journey in this form. The news struck harder than any loss I had borne—not because death is ever easy, but because his departure carried a weight of despair I could not fully fathom. I knew then the coffin was his, not mine, and the shadow of my own end lifted, leaving only grief in its wake.

A week before he passed, our group of psychotherapists gathered at the dojo. Jim did not appear—an absence others brushed aside, but I felt his leaving deep within me, a hollow ache that pulled me apart from the rest. I left them to their discussions and stepped alone into the garden, settling onto a bench Jim had loved, a spot I now call Jim's bench. There, surrounded by the quiet rustle of leaves, I sat with his absence, sensing a farewell I could not yet name. I placed flowers in his empty chair inside, an unexplainable gesture that felt right.

Weeks later, after his death, we gathered once more for a memorial in that same space. I placed flowers there again, a silent tribute to the man who had walked beside me, opening doors within my soul I had not dared to open alone.

Days later, I sat on Jim's bench in my front garden, sobbing into the stillness, and whispered, "Jim, I need a sign you are still near." Instantly, a rainbow arched across the sky—bold, radiant, a thread of light piercing my grief. I gasped, my breath caught, tears halted by its sudden glow. It was no mere chance, but a gift—a radiant reminder of love's reach beyond the veil, as clear as the chimes of Papa's clock or my brother's laughter from the other side. I had never seen a rainbow over my house before—it appeared at the exact moment of my plea. The name of the bridge he had chosen for his departure—Rainbow Bridge—struck me as a profound synchronicity, a message that left no doubt: I am still with you, just in another way.

I needed to travel north to see Jim's wife, to offer what comfort I could in our shared grief. Recognizing my need for self-care during this most difficult time, I searched online for accommodations and found a guest house that offered not just a place to stay, but a therapy called Watsu—a practice where you float in a warm pool while being held in silence and gentle movement in the water. The thought of being held in silence spoke to something deep within me, as I had no words for what I was feeling; the grief was overwhelming, and I had no desire to talk to anyone.

On that journey, I believe Jim guided me still, gently nudging me toward the guest house where I had arranged to stay—a place of quiet nestled in snow-draped hills. There, I met Giovanni, a man whose presence would weave love's surrender ever deeper into my life for the next seven years—a profound influence born of this challenging crossing.

Before leaving the area, I drove to Rainbow Bridge, the place where Jim had leapt. Snow swirled around me, the air biting and cold, yet my sadness cloaked me so fully that I scarcely felt the freeze. I stood at the edge, praying, and released five feathers in his honor—three owl feathers for the sensitive boy he had been, wounded at seven by his mother's loss, and two eagle feathers for the man he became, soaring now to her arms.

The owl feathers swirled beneath the bridge, lingering in the water as if held by an unseen hand, a curious energy attempting to soften the wound of his departure. The eagle feathers floated down the river, free and swift, a symbol of flight beyond pain. I watched, my breath a quiet prayer, trusting that Jim had found peace in a reunion I could only imagine. That bridge, named for rainbows, bore witness to both his end and his beginning—a synchronicity too deep for words.

Today, as I reflect on Jim's journey, I reach to celebrate the wonder, resilience, and power of the human spirit to rise out of suffering into new life. I reach for hope. I reach for faith. I celebrate the beauty of another communion—birth, death, resurrection, transformation. Divine Grace.

Jim's leaving taught me surrender anew—not to change what I could not, but to stand with it, to trust love's persistence even in the darkest valleys. His heart, his laugh, his violin's song remain woven into mine, a mentor whose lessons linger in the silence. My time with Jim profoundly shaped my later work as a healer and medium, teaching me that true healing often comes not through words but through a quality of presence—a presence of love that transcends technique. Perhaps you have known such a farewell—a loss that carves a space for light, a sign that defies farewell. For me, this was a heart's farewell, a surrender to love's eternal pulse—a peace I offer now to you.

INVITATION TO PAUSE

- Consider someone whose presence profoundly shaped your inner life. What gifts did they leave you and how do those gifts continue to influence who you are becoming?
- Reflect on a farewell that changed you. What grace was hidden in that parting? And if you could speak to their soul today, what would you say? Allow your answer to rise not from the mind, but from the heart.
- Where in your life have you experienced signs or synchronicities that felt like messages from beyond? How did those experiences change your understanding of love's persistence?
- Think about times when your body has carried grief or trauma that needed to move through you. What did you learn about the wisdom of surrender in those moments?
- How might honoring both the pain and the beauty of profound loss open you to deeper capacity for love and presence with others?

HEALING BEYOND TOUCH

"The body is the most visible layer of light—
but the soul stretches far beyond what can be touched."

In 2007, I found myself in Hawaii, participating in advanced training in Rolf Structural Integration with my teacher, Emmett Hutchins. Emmett was not just any instructor—he was a living treasure in the Structural Integration community, one of Dr. Ida Rolf's first appointed teachers alongside Peter Melchior. These two men were pioneers and masters of the work Dr. Rolf had developed, carrying her legacy forward with unwavering dedication. To learn from Emmett was to receive the transmission of knowledge directly from its source, a lineage of understanding passed from hand to hand, heart to heart.

The six-week advanced training was intense, immersing us in the deep principles of Dr. Rolf's work. We explored her fundamental understanding that "an effective human being is a whole that is greater than the sum of its parts"—a philosophy that underscores how the body's well-being involves not just physical alignment but the integration of all aspects of the individual. One afternoon, as we were discussing subtle aspects of technique, Emmett mentioned something that sent a ripple of concern through me and the other practitioners present. He was experiencing tremendous trouble with his wrists—the very instruments through which he had channeled healing for decades. At seventy years old, after a lifetime of this demanding physical work, his body was signaling limitations that might force him to retire.

"I'm not sure how much longer I can continue," he confided, his usually confident voice tinged with a rare vulnerability. The thought of losing Emmett's contribution to the field was devastating. His understanding of Dr. Rolf's work went beyond technique; he embodied the philosophy, the artistry, and the intuitive dimensions that made Structural Integration transformative rather than merely therapeutic.

Later that week, to my surprise and honor, Emmett asked if I might work with him to help ease the trouble in his wrists. This request—from a master to a student—was both humbling and intimidating. Twice a week for the remainder of the training, I would arrive at Emmett's office at the appointed hour, ready to offer sessions to the very person who had taught me the work.

The sessions progressed well, and Emmett experienced noticeable relief. His hands, which had guided so many bodies toward better alignment with gravity, were themselves beginning to find ease. On the final day of the training, as I was preparing to depart, Emmett asked if I could offer one more session.

"I'm sorry, Emmett," I apologized. "I'm catching a plane home in just an hour."

As I turned to leave, a thought suddenly crystallized—a whisper from beyond my mind. I recalled Dr. Rolf's teaching that we should "go around the problem; get the system sufficiently resilient so that it is able to change, and it will change. It doesn't have to be forced." Perhaps there was another way to approach Emmett's healing.

"Emmett," I said, pausing at his door, "what do you think about continuing the sessions in the field, energetically?"

He smiled, his eyes lighting with curiosity and openness—qualities

that had likely made him such a receptive student to Dr. Rolf's revolu-
tionary ideas decades earlier. "Sure," he replied, "That's a great idea."

AND SO BEGAN an experiment that would challenge and expand my
understanding of healing work. For several months following, Emmett
in Hawaii and I in California would "meet" every Tuesday afternoon. At
the appointed time, I would lie down on my treatment table and work
with Emmett energetically from my office in California. I approached
these sessions exactly as I would an in-person treatment, moving
methodically through the patterns and protocols of Structural Integration, feeling for restrictions and imbalances, and facilitating release, all
without physical contact.

To my surprise, these distance sessions proved effective. Emmett
reported continued improvement in his wrists, which allowed him to
postpone thoughts of retirement. As the weeks passed, I discovered that
not only could I sense and shift patterns within the connective tissue of
Emmett's body, but I was also working from the inside out, accessing
the energetic blueprint beneath the physical form. This experience
embodied Dr. Rolf's insight that restoring the elasticity and sliding
capacity of the fascia allows the body to function with more ease and
efficiency. But I discovered that this restoration could happen through
multiple avenues of entry into the body's universe.

One night, several months into our distance work, a strange pull
tugged me awake from a deep sleep, and I spontaneously began working
with Emmett energetically—something that had never occurred before.
Until then, our sessions had always been scheduled and intentional.
After a short time, I caught myself: "What are you doing working on
Emmett now? You don't have an appointment with him in the middle
of the night. Go back to sleep," I scolded myself.

I returned to sleep but soon found myself in the grip of the most
terrible nightmare I had ever experienced. In the dream, I was a young
child, perhaps ten years old, being held down by my wrists on a hospital
table. I was choking to death on my own blood, unable to move,

gripped by absolute terror. The experience was so horrific that I woke up trembling, heart pounding in my chest.

As I lay in the darkness, trying to calm my breathing, a realization dawned slowly but with absolute certainty: this was not my nightmare. This was Emmett's experience I had somehow accessed. The conviction was unshakable, though it defied logical explanation.

Following this insight, I made the intention to return to sleep and re-enter the nightmare, but this time with awareness. I would go back to tell Emmett he was not alone. As I drifted back into the dream state, I again saw the operating table, the panicked medical staff holding down a boy by his wrists as they struggled to control a critical situation. But this time, I also perceived the presence of light surrounding the scene—angels, guardians, beings of compassion, witnessing and holding the space with love. I felt a profound sense of peace replace the terror, knowing the boy was not alone and would ultimately be safe. The light glowed softly, a silent promise that echoed across time and space—"you were never alone, you are not alone, you will never be alone."

A week passed before I found the courage to share this extraordinary experience with Emmett. When I finally described the nightmare during our next scheduled session, his response left me breathless.

"That actually happened to me when I was a boy," he confirmed quietly. "I was having my tonsils removed, and I moved unexpectedly. The surgeon accidentally cut my throat, and I nearly died. They had to hold me down by my wrists to stop the bleeding and save my life."

The implication was staggering. Emmett's body had held this trauma for over sixty years, the fear and helplessness embedded in the very tissues of his wrists—the same wrists now causing him pain and threatening to end his career as a practitioner and teacher. The body's memory, it seemed, was far more tenacious than conscious recollection. This aligned perfectly with Dr. Rolf's holistic approach, which recognized that the body's well-being involves the integration of mental and emotional aspects, not just physical alignment.

Most remarkable of all was what happened after this shared recognition of the trauma: within days, Emmett's wrist pain disappeared completely. The energetic work had accessed what hands-on manipulation alone could not reach—the emotional imprint of trauma stored in tissue memory. Once witnessed and released in the field, the physical symptoms resolved.

THIS EXPERIENCE TRANSFORMED my understanding of Dr. Rolf's work and healing in general. It validated her vision that "there's no such thing as metaphysics, there is only the physics we've not yet discovered." The boundaries between physical and energetic healing, between touch and distant work, between past and present trauma—all revealed themselves as more permeable than our conventional models suggest.

Today, distance healing forms an integral part of my practice. When I work with clients this way, I invite them to begin with "the intention of openness, receiving the energy healing into your field... and just notice—notice your breath, notice the space, notice the freedom, or anything else that arises in the moment."

I believe, as Dr. Rolf did, that "the appropriate integration of the bodies of man in the gravity field is a long-term evolutionary project." Our work with the physical form is ultimately about aligning with greater fields of energy and consciousness. The experience with Emmett showed me that healing can flow between practitioner and recipient across any distance when guided by clear intention and deep presence. *A field where love bridges all gaps.*

Emmett Hutchins passed away peacefully, leaving behind a profound legacy of healing and teaching. I believe his influence in my life began long before our physical meeting. The transmission he shared lives on through every client who receives this work, as I remain dedicated to perpetuating the traditional teachings of Dr. Ida P. Rolf, just as my teacher did before me—now through spiritual mediumship and distant healing. Dr. Rolf recognized that the body's universe can be entered and transformed through various means, with physical hands-on techniques being just one of many effective approaches.

INVITATION TO PAUSE

- Have you ever sensed a connection with someone beyond words or physical presence? What did those moments teach you about the invisible threads that link us all?

- Consider a mentor, teacher, or guide whose presence shaped your path. What wisdom did they pass to you—through silence, through being, through their example?

- Reflect on a memory or moment when you felt healing begin, not from fixing or forcing, but from being truly seen and witnessed. How did that experience of being held in loving presence create space for transformation?

- Where might old pain or unhealed experiences be held? What would it mean to approach these places with the same gentle witnessing presence rather than trying to force change?

- How do you carry forward the legacy of those who have profoundly influenced your life? In what ways can you offer that same field of healing presence to yourself—or to someone else—today?

THROUGH A LOVER'S EYES

"True love does not come to complete us—it comes
to reveal the light we've always carried within."

In my fiftieth year, after Jim's passing left me adrift in a sea of vulnerability, life unfolded a gift I had never sought—romantic love, tender and unbidden. It bloomed where I had once planted only devotion to spirit. Jim's departure had dissolved the boundaries I had constructed around my spiritual life, revealing how I had allowed a spiritual bypass to take root.

I began to see how certain religious frameworks had potentially masked or complicated my authentic spiritual development. The church's teachings—original sin, guilt, confessions—had fed directly into patterns of self-doubt and shame, a subtle reinforcement of not being good enough. I recognized then how I had used spiritual practices to avoid dealing with difficult emotions and psychological wounds. I had envisioned a path of service, my heart pledged to God alone, yet these walls could no longer contain the vastness I felt stirring within me.

This realization added an important layer to my journey toward a more integrated spirituality, one that would eventually find expression through a deeper and more transparent love. I stepped away, uncertain but trusting, into a season of quiet unraveling.

It was then I returned to the guest house nestled in snow-draped hills, a sanctuary I had first found in the wake of Jim's loss. There, in the warm water pool, Giovanni held me in silence, his presence a steady anchor as my body trembled. I believe those shudders rose from memories of my birth—a trauma etched deep in my cells, beyond the reach of words. For years, psychotherapy had offered insight, yet in those two years with Giovanni, something deeper unwound. Without explanation, without demand, he allowed my body to unfold its ancient wounds. The warm water cradled me, his hands gentle and unwavering, and I surrendered to a healing more profound than all the talking I had ever done. Each tremble released a thread of fear, each sigh a whisper of freedom. In these moments of wordless healing, I began to sense that this connection was not leading me away from my spiritual path but rather toward its more authentic expression—as if the divine I had sought in meditation and prayer was now reaching for me through the compassionate touch of another human being.

Giovanni, his English sweetened by his native Italian accent, carried the warmth of the Mediterranean in his manner: unhurried, sensual, present. He was an experienced sailor who had crossed the Atlantic three times, and an amazing chef who prepared pasta like an artist in love, like poetry and music, his hands moving with the same confidence whether kneading dough or caressing my skin. When he cooked, he sang, his voice filling our shared space with melodies from his homeland.

Our connection grew beyond the pool's embrace. We walked together along quiet paths, swam in the nearby lake, our silences as rich as our shared words. Time softened me, and gradually, a realization dawned—we were falling in love. Giovanni moved with exquisite care, always seeking permission, his pace a reverence I had never known. I wondered, curious and open, what it might feel like to fall in love at fifty, my first love. I had never held such a thought before; my life's compass had pointed only toward divine service. This love was different —a quiet unfolding, a surrender not to an ideal, but to a man who stood before me, flawed and real. Gradually, I understood that this love was not separate from my spiritual journey but rather its natural evolution, as if my years of devotion had prepared me for this more embodied experience of the divine.

The intimacy that followed deepened my understanding of surrender beyond anything I had imagined. Having no experience, everything was new to me—the feeling of his skin against mine, the tender exploration of a kiss. One night, after passionate love, he gazed into my eyes, his silence a mirror. I asked, my voice trembling, "What are you looking at?" He offered no words, only continued to look, and in that stillness, I saw what he saw. Through a lover's eyes, I saw I was worthy, and that I embodied that essence of love I had encountered during my experiences beyond the threshold of death. In that recognition, I glimpsed something eternal—that the "I" of who we are is not confined to our personal stories, but is a living expression of the One Universal Infinite Love itself. Each of us, a unique spark of that boundless consciousness, incarnate in flesh yet not limited by it. His gaze reflected not just my individual worth, but the divine presence we each carry—the I AM that transcends yet embraces our human journey. His touch, patient and unguarded, gradually melted defenses I had carried since childhood. I surrendered, not in grand gestures, but in the quiet moments—his hand on mine, his breath against my skin, our separate selves dissolving into that greater wholeness.

We dreamed together, purchasing a forty-foot sailboat that we planned to restore, imagining voyages across vast waters, horizons unlimited before us. We worked side by side, sanding, painting, rewiring —creating a vessel for adventures we would share. Though we never sailed the high seas, we experienced smaller journeys, the water beneath us a gentle reminder of where we began.

Our love flourished for four years, a tender dance of presence and acceptance. Then, a shadow fell—cancer claimed his body, slowly dimming the strength I had come to cherish.

As seasons passed, I noticed subtle changes—a lingering fatigue after our walks, a hesitation in his movements once fluid as water. When the diagnosis came, it fell between us like a stone in still water, ripples extending outward, touching everything. Our love didn't diminish, but transformed—from the passionate dance of new lovers to the sacred waltz of caregiver and beloved. His body, once my harbor, gradually became the vessel I tended with reverent hands. In this new chapter, I discovered that love contains multitudes—it can be both fire and gentle rain, exhilaration and patient endurance.

The following three years transformed our love into a different form. One of the most challenging aspects was losing him little by little. I had loved lying next to him, feeling his body against mine, but as the cancer progressed, even this simple pleasure became impossible. He weighed less than a hundred pounds before he passed, his once-vital frame diminished. Yet even in this painful diminishment, love revealed itself. Love cannot be lost; it is the one truth that remains when all else falls away. In losing him, I discovered that love never dies—it simply finds new ways to speak to the heart.

I nursed him, this beautiful man who had held me in water and silence, now fragile in my arms. He told me once, as his voice grew faint, "No one has ever received me so fully. I am grateful the last person in my life loved me just as I am, never asking me to be different." His words pierced me—a gift of gratitude I carry still. I accepted him fully, as he had me, and in that mutual surrender, we found a sacred space where love needed no alteration. In these moments of caregiving, I recognized that this was not separate from my spiritual practice but was, in fact, its purest manifestation—love expressed through service, presence, and unconditional acceptance.

He passed in my arms, his breath a final sigh against my chest, seven years after we first met.

After Giovanni's passing, I returned once more to water—that element where our love had first awakened. In the warm pool where he had once held me through my trembling, I now allowed my grief to flow. Each tear a testament to what we had shared, each breath a reminder that love outlasts physical presence. My essence, deepened by having known the divine through human touch, expanded to hold both joy and sorrow as sacred. Grief moved through me like those early tremors, releasing not trauma now but attachment, teaching me that loving and losing are not separate acts but one continuous surrender. In time, I came to feel Giovanni's presence not as absence but as essence—infused in morning light, in the scent of fresh pasta, in the gentle rocking of water against the shore.

I feel fortunate. Many never know a love so tender, so revealing. To be seen through a lover's eyes is a rare gift—a mirror reflecting worth without condition. Many never have the chance to experience such a connection, one that reveals love as both a giving and a receiving. Giovanni's gaze taught me I am lovable; his touch was a bridge to a surrender I had once reserved for spirit alone. Now, I understand that love's pulse weaves through all things—human and divine, fleeting and eternal.

At fifty, I had discovered that it's never too late for love to reshape your understanding of surrender. Through Giovanni, I learned that the deepest spiritual truths can sometimes be found not in monastery walls or sacred texts, but in the silent gaze of a lover who sees you completely and loves what they see. Far from diverting me from my spiritual path, this love had brought me into a more authentic relationship with the divine—one expressed through human touch, daily presence, and the sacred act of witnessing another's being in all its flawed perfection. It revealed that the divine I had sought in prayer and silence had been seeking me through the language of human connection all along.

This is the sacred alchemy that transforms personal love, revealing it as a gateway to the universal—a brilliant facet of the same diamond of consciousness that illuminates all creation. In this crucible of intimacy, what begins as connection between two souls expands into revelations about our shared divine nature.

Perhaps you have known such a love—a surrender that shifts the soul's foundation, a gift that lingers beyond farewell. In these moments of genuine connection, we glimpse our true nature beyond the separate self, touching that infinite love that is our shared essence. For me, this was a heart's awakening, teaching me that love, in all its forms, is the ultimate path of surrender. I still feel graced by the gift of such a love—a love that revealed itself as the truest expression of the spiritual devotion I had sought all along, reminding me that we are never separate from the love that sustains us.

INVITATION TO PAUSE

- Have you ever been seen—truly seen—by someone who loved you just as you are? What did their gaze awaken in you? What parts of yourself softened in the presence of that love?
- Consider a moment when love felt like a homecoming, not just of the heart, but of the soul. Did it awaken something within you—something sacred, something true?
- Think about the different forms love takes—passionate, nurturing, friendship, caregiving. How has love transformed in your own life, and what has each form taught you about surrender?
- Let yourself sit with the memory of a love that revealed your worthiness. Allow whatever arises to move through you—not as thought, but as feeling, as remembrance, as love remembering itself.
- Reflect on self-love—do you see yourself through a lover's eyes? You are that beloved.

THE STICK AND STILLNESS

"Do nothing, and the next moment finds you anyway."

I walked toward the meditation hall in the early morning chill, the air crisp around me as darkness still held the world in silence. My cold breath mingled with the faint scent of incense as I stepped inside. It was my first time practicing Zen under my Aikido sensei. In this space, he held the quiet authority of a Rinzai Zen master. I had long met the divine in the stillness of meditation and prayer, but this was a surrender stripped of form—asking only for presence.

This was our routine—Zen meditation before dawn, followed by morning Aikido practice, then breakfast together.

I was not alone in this initiation. Several of my own Aikido students had joined me, curious about the connection between the moving meditation of Aikido and the stillness of Zen practice. I felt both teacher and student in that moment—guiding them into an experience I had yet to fully understand myself.

Inside, the hall was dimly lit, the glow of a single candle flickering in the stillness. The silence was profound, thick with something unspoken yet deeply understood. One by one, we entered, each taking a mat and a small pillow, moving as if guided by an invisible rhythm. Without a word, we arranged ourselves in a square formation, all facing inward toward the center.

Then, the bell rang— a deep, resonant tone that seemed to stretch beyond time itself. The shift in energy was immediate—everyone straightened their posture, the room alive with presence. With that sound, an invisible boundary was crossed—now, required stillness was the practice. Even if a fly were to land on your nose, you were not to move. To break this discipline was to break the sacred container of the practice itself.

As I settled into this required stillness, my awareness expanded, taking in the details: the weight of my body, the distant sound of wind against the wooden walls, the faint creak of someone adjusting their seat —a final movement before surrendering to complete stillness.

And then, I saw him.

A figure moved through the center—slow, deliberate, precise. The Jikijitsu. He carried a long wooden stick, the Kyosaku—what I would later learn was called the "encouragement" or "awakening" stick. But in that moment, my only thought was, "If he comes near me with that stick, I will break it over his head."

The thought surprised me. It wasn't fear—it was the warrior in me instantly on alert. Though I had practiced meditation for many years, the experience of someone walking around with a big stick triggered my martial instincts. I laugh now thinking about how ready I was for battle in that silent meditation hall. The Jikijitsu and his stick awakened zanshin—continuous awareness—I certainly was awake, and my body was poised for action, even as stillness was the practice.

The Jikijitsu moved with unwavering presence, passing each student, pausing occasionally. When he reached someone in need of correction—whether drowsy, tense, or unfocused—he would touch their shoulder with the stick. If they leaned forward in acknowledgment, a swift yet precise strike would land between their shoulder blades

—not punishment, but awakening. This ritual exchange was the only motion permitted after the bell.

From my place in the square, I caught sight of Michael, one of my most dedicated students. His face betrayed nothing, but I knew him well enough to sense his confusion. When the Jikijitsu approached him, Michael—unaware of the protocol—bowed his head slightly, a gesture of respect learned from our Aikido practice. The Jikijitsu took this as the traditional request for correction and delivered a sharp, crisp strike with the Kyosaku.

I watched Michael's eyes widen, his body straightening with the sudden jolt. For a moment, I thought he might break discipline—stand up or speak, shattering the sacred silence of the zendo. Instead, something remarkable happened. His face shifted from surprise to understanding, then to a kind of surrender. He settled deeper into his posture, his breath visibly steadying while his body remained perfectly still. Without knowing the tradition, he had accidentally invited the very awakening the practice offered, and then embraced it fully within the strict container of complete stillness.

I sat, waiting.

Would the Jikijitsu stop near me? Would I allow myself to be corrected while maintaining the perfect stillness demanded by tradition?

Minutes stretched into eternity. My legs fell asleep, but I did not move. My mind darted between thoughts, but I stayed still. I breathed. I let go. Remaining absolutely motionless became its own lesson in surrender.

As we sat, the morning sunrise gradually changed the light in the hall, casting golden rays through paper screens. Dust particles danced in the air like tiny stars, and the wooden floor planks transformed from shadow to amber as the light crept across their surface. The space transformed in silent glory, reminiscent of that luminous stillness I had experienced beyond the threshold of death as an infant—a memory of surrender before I had words to name it.

He never struck me that morning. But something shifted within me regardless.

At breakfast after the first Aikido morning practice, Michael approached me, his bowl of rice steaming in the cool air.

"Sensei," he said quietly, "I wasn't expecting that."

I just laughed—a genuine, spontaneous response that said more than any wise teaching could have in that moment.

"But it wasn't what I thought," he continued. "It wasn't punishment. It was..." he searched for the words, "...like being reminded that I'm here. Really here."

His insight struck me more powerfully than any Kyosaku could have. In his accidental surrender, Michael had discovered the essence of the practice more quickly than my calculated resistance would allow. The student is often my teacher.

That first Zen meditation, with its candlelit silence, its requirement for perfect stillness, and the slow footsteps of the Jikijitsu, stayed with me long after the sun had risen. It was a lesson not in stillness alone, but in meeting resistance with curiosity, in surrendering to something greater than my own expectations.

My teacher's approach had always blended these elements seamlessly. In his broken English—he was Japanese—he would often say, "Don't think, just do." That morning with the Jikijitsu, I understood what he meant in a new way. The alertness I felt wasn't separate from the meditation; it was part of it. Mushin—no mind—and zanshin—continuous awareness—weren't just concepts from our Aikido training. They were living realities in that candlelit hall.

Sitting zazen became a beautiful addition to my Aikido practice, a perfect complement to the flowing movements on the mat. Together, they formed another layer in my lifelong exploration of surrender. Teaching me that true power emerges not from control but from yielding to something greater.

Some time later, I had the opportunity to stay at one of the oldest Japanese Soto Zen monasteries in the United States, where the practice offered a slightly different approach. There, practitioners faced the wall rather than the center, emphasizing shikantaza—"just sitting," a form of open awareness meditation. This experience further deepened my understanding of the different paths to the same truth of inner stillness.

When I first met my Aikido teacher, he invited me to sit on the floor and have tea. I remember him saying, "The most important thing is to be yourself." Those simple words carried profound wisdom that has stayed with me through decades of practice. To me, this has meant being the authentic aspect of oneself. My greatest hope is that as a teacher today, I might be so transparent that essence, the divine presence, shines through.

Later, when I shared my warrior response with the Jikijitsu—how I had been ready to break the stick over his head if he approached—he nodded with approval. "That is exactly the type of alertness we are looking for," he said. Perhaps my instinctive reaction wasn't so far from the practice's intention after all.

The discipline of mushin and zanshin, learned through Aikido and Zen, became foundational in my later practice of spiritual mediumship. The discipline of emptying myself—of becoming a vessel rather than a controller of the message—allows me to bridge worlds just as zazen bridges action and stillness. When receiving messages from beyond, I return to my teacher's words: "Don't think, just do." The warrior's alertness, the meditator's stillness, and the medium's openness—all expressions of the same profound surrender I have been learning since my first breath.

INVITATION TO PAUSE

- What does it mean to you to "do nothing"—not in passivity, but in presence? How might this kind of alert stillness transform your relationship with action and reaction?
- Consider times when your initial resistance to something led to unexpected insight or awakening.
- Reflect on the balance between warrior alertness and meditative stillness in your own life. Where do you need

more zanshin—continuous awareness—and where might you benefit from mushin—acting without overthought?

- Think about how being "corrected" or challenged has sometimes served as awakening rather than punishment. What would it mean to welcome such moments as opportunities for presence?

- Sit quietly with the question of authentic being. Let your breath guide you. Allow awareness to arise—not as thought, but as spacious presence, where stillness becomes its own form of knowing.

ANCIENT WAYS

"Creation is already whole—
our task is to return to harmony with it."

The river's song greeted me each morning as I walked with Tundra, my silver-gray wolf dog, along the banks near my small mountain home. In my early thirties, as I pursued graduate studies, we had found sanctuary in the Sierra Nevada Mountains of California, where I had rented a modest house that offered the quiet and solitude I needed. By day, I immersed myself in textbooks—Exercise Physiology and Marriage and Family Therapy—two master's programs I pursued simultaneously, crafting my own path toward holistic healing when no formal somatic psychology programs yet existed. By dawn and dusk, the river and forest became my classroom, teaching lessons no university could provide.

It was on one of these morning walks that Tundra's ears perked up, fixing on something ahead. My faithful companion, his deep brown eyes wiser than most, often sensed what I could not—especially when it came to the unseen. Two dogs appeared from around the bend, then another, followed by a man with weathered skin and calm, observant eyes. Tundra approached the dogs cautiously, then broke into playful chasing. As the animals created their own communion, I smiled at his intuitive ability to sense the energy of others—a gift that had guided me through many situations over our years together. The man and I began to talk.

"The name's Bear," he said simply, extending a hand calloused from work but gentle in its grip.

Our conversations began casually—comments about the weather, the dogs, the changing seasons. Over time, I shared my work as a Rolf Structural Integration therapist and my studies. "I am interested in healing," I told him, "but not in the allopathic, symptom-based model. I am looking for something more whole, more connected. That is why I am cobbling together these different disciplines. Someday I hope to open a wellness center that honors the whole person."

Bear would nod, listening more than speaking. Weeks passed in this way, our morning encounters becoming a ritual as reliable as the sunrise. Then one morning, as we watched the mist rise from the river, he turned to me and said, "I am a healer—the Cherokee medicine way."

The words hung between us, simple yet profound. In that moment, a door opened to an ancient lineage of healing wisdom I had sensed but never accessed. Bear specialized in healing prayer and served as a sweat lodge leader. He offered to teach me if I was willing to learn.

"The healing ways of my people are not secret," he explained. "They are sacred. There's a difference. Secret means keeping knowledge to yourself. Sacred means approaching knowledge with reverence. Are you ready to learn with reverence?"

I was. True to his word, Bear's teachings honored both the sacred and the practical. In the months that followed, Bear became my teacher, guiding me into the healing traditions of his Cherokee ancestors. He showed me how to use sage and tobacco in prayer, how words, stories, and songs could carry healing intention. He taught me to recognize the energy of animals, plants, and elements—to draw upon their strength not through dominance but through respect and relationship.

"Everything you need for healing is already here," he would say, gesturing to the forest around us. "The Creator has provided it all. Our job is to remember how to listen, how to ask permission, how to give thanks."

One spring day, as the river ran high with snowmelt, Bear suggested we build a sweat lodge near my home. "It is time you learn the ceremony from the inside," he said. We spent weeks preparing, gathering young willow branches from along the riverbank, asking permission from each plant and offering tobacco in gratitude. The ground near the river was soft sand, perfect for sinking the branches to form the skeleton of the round lodge, which we then covered with heavy cloth tarps.

"Now we need the right stones," Bear instructed. "Not just any rock will do. We need ones that can withstand the heat without cracking or exploding."

We searched the riverbed and surrounding hills, selecting stones with care. Bear taught me to approach each one with a question rather than an assumption: "Are you willing to serve in the lodge?" Some, he said, would say no, and these we left in place with gratitude for their honesty.

When the lodge was complete, Bear showed me how to prepare the fire that would heat the stones, a process that took most of a day. Everything was done with reverence—the gathering of wood, the building of the fire, the placement of the stones. As dusk approached, the stones glowed red-hot in the fire pit, ready to be carried into the lodge with antler tools and placed in the central pit.

In the dim light of early evening, Bear led the first ceremony, teaching me the protocols, the songs, the prayers, the way to pour water over the heated stones to create steam. The darkness inside the lodge was complete, the heat intense. As I sat cross-legged on the earth, sweat streaming down my body, Bear's voice rose in Cherokee prayer, then translated:

"We give thanks to the stones, our oldest ancestors who hold the memory of all that has been. We give thanks to the water, which gives life to all beings. We give thanks to the fire, which transforms and purifies. We give

thanks to the plants that form our lodge and heal our bodies. We give thanks to the directions—East where the sun rises, South where life flourishes, West where the sun sets, North where wisdom dwells. We pray for healing for all who enter this lodge, for all relations, for Mother Earth herself."

The ceremony lasted for hours, alternating between intense heat as water met stone and brief respites when the lodge flap was opened between rounds. In that sacred darkness, I experienced healing prayer in a way I never had before—embodied, elemental, ancient yet immediate. I emerged exhausted yet cleansed, my mind quieter than it had been in years.

In the months that followed, we held small gatherings at the lodge, inviting those who sought healing. Bear guided the ceremonies while teaching me the proper way to lead. He showed me drumming patterns to shift consciousness, plaintive flute notes to open the heart, and how to preserve and use feathers—particularly those of the ghost owl and hawk—to carry prayers skyward.

"The energy of the bird remains in the feather," he explained. "Their spirit helps your prayers take flight."

This teaching was put to the test when I received an urgent call about a friend who had been hospitalized with severe cramping throughout his body. When I arrived, he was writhing in pain, screaming as waves of cramps seized him. Tests had revealed he was bleeding internally—nearly two pints gone—his condition deteriorating rapidly. But nothing could be done until the doctor arrived.

As nurses looked on with a mixture of curiosity and skepticism, I took out the owl feathers and sage Bear had given me. I began to pray in the way I had been taught, moving the feather gently around my friend's body while encouraging him to breathe with me. Gradually, his breathing synchronized with mine, slowing and deepening. The tension in his face began to ease, the cramping subsided, and the pain receded to a tolerable level. It bought precious time until doctors could begin blood transfusions. One nurse pulled me aside afterward, whispering, "I do not know what you just did, but I have never seen anything like it."

Bear later nodded when I told him what had happened. "You are learning," was all he said, but his eyes held approval.

My education expanded when Bear introduced me to the Tule River Indian Reservation. Once a month, we would make the two hour journey to participate in their sweat lodge ceremonies. I felt profoundly grateful to be welcomed into these sacred traditions, to learn from tribal elders whose knowledge had been passed down through countless generations. These were not performances for outsiders but living ceremonies —a privilege I never took for granted.

It was during this period of deep immersion in Native American healing traditions that an unexpected opportunity arose: a chance to visit Machu Picchu with a small group, guided by a Quechuan medicine man. Something stirred within me at the prospect—a recognition, perhaps, that my healing journey was about to cross continents, connecting indigenous wisdom across North and South America in ways I could not yet foresee.

As I prepared for the journey, Bear offered a simple blessing: "Go with open eyes and an empty cup. The mountains have much to teach those who know how to listen." Little did I know that his teachings about approaching wisdom with reverence would prove essential preparation for the indigenous traditions awaiting me across continents, or how the Andean spirits would whisper secrets that would transform my understanding of healing forever.

INVITATION TO PAUSE

- What does it mean to you that healing is not something to be achieved, but remembered? How might this shift your approach to your own wellness and wholeness?
- Consider finding your way to nature—standing barefoot on the earth, being still. As you breathe with the land, can you feel her heartbeat beneath your feet?

- Reflect on the sacred wisdom you have received—not from books or teachers, but from the land, the animals, from the silence within. What has nature taught you that no classroom could?
- Where in your life might you need to shift from seeking knowledge to approaching it with reverence? What would change if you saw healing as returning to harmony rather than fixing what's broken?
- Let the knowing rise—not as thought, but as relationship, as reverence, as wholeness remembered.

ANDEAN WHISPER

"I disappeared into the stillness,
and the mountain held what was left of me."

With Bear's blessing resonating in my heart, I felt called to embark on a journey that would weave together ancient wisdom traditions across continents. But first, I needed to return to my roots—to Ojai, California, where my grandmother's Chumash heritage had planted the first seeds of my connection to indigenous ways. In this small valley nestled within the Topatopa Mountains, I would gather sacred soil before setting out for Peru.

I stood on my grandmother's modest porch, built by my grandfather's hands, and gazed up at the surrounding mountains just as she had done countless times. "There is snow on the Chief this morning," she would say, pointing to the mountain whose contours formed the distinct profile of a Native American chief's head with his feathered headdress. The memory of her voice—and her reverence for the land—filled me with a sense of continuity and purpose.

Ojai means "little nest" in Chumash, an apt name for this valley cradled by mountains. In my childhood, it was simple—one post office, one grocery store, one coffee shop—before Hollywood discovered its quiet beauty and altered its character. Yet its essence remained: Ojai rests atop an energy vortex, where the magnetic pull of the mountains and the crossing of ley lines create a palpable spiritual vibration.

The Chumash people understood this power. For over 13,000 years, they inhabited this coastal region in direct relationship with the land, the natural world, and the universe beyond. They recognized spirit in all things—from the humblest stone to the stars overhead. Their shamans were healers, astronomers, and community leaders who drew strength from the sacred mountains flanking the Ojai valley—just as I now sought to do.

What pulled me back to Ojai before Peru was something I had recently learned: Ojai's mountains were said to be the "daughter mountains" of Machu Picchu. This spiritual kinship between my birthplace and my destination felt undeniable—a connection I could not ignore. Both had endured similar wounds: the Chumash decimated by Spanish conquest, just as the Inca had been in Peru. Both held ancient wisdom, largely forgotten. Both called to me.

I decided to hike to the mountain we called "the Chief"—to offer prayers and gather a small amount of soil—a gift from daughter to mother mountain that I would carry to Machu Picchu. The trail was steep, winding through chaparral and oak, occasionally opening to reveal the valley below, unfolding like a patchwork quilt of orchards and humble homes.

At the summit, I sat in meditation. The wind whispered through the scrub brush, carrying scents of sage and dust. I closed my eyes, and a vision came—Chumash people moving through these same mountains centuries ago, gathering herbs, hunting, praying. Then the vision darkened: disease, missions, the slow unraveling of a sacred way of life. The parallels with Peru were unmistakable—the same colonizing force, the same pattern of destruction, echoing across thousands of miles.

I opened my medicine bag and carefully placed a small amount of soil inside, wrapping it in red cloth. With it, I would carry prayers of healing—not just for the Chumash and Quechua peoples, but for the deeper wound that colonization had carved across the Americas. As Bear had taught me, true healing must reach the root of suffering, not merely soothe its symptoms. This conquest had been not only physical and cultural—it had been spiritual.

As I descended the mountain, a quiet clarity settled in. I was not going to Peru merely as a student or observer, but as a bridge—a vessel to help reconnect spiritual lineages fractured by shared historical wounds. The soil in my medicine bag was more than a symbolic gesture; it was a commitment—to remembrance, to reverence, to healing across time and place.

When I finally boarded the plane for Peru, my medicine bag held close against my heart, I carried not only the teachings of Bear and the Tule River Tribe, but also the spirit of my birthplace and its enduring wisdom. I didn't know exactly how these threads would weave together, but I trusted the path unfolding before me—a path that had begun long before my birth and would continue long after I was gone.

The flight to Peru felt like crossing a threshold—not just into another country, but into an ancient memory waiting to be awakened. As the plane descended toward Cusco, the ancient capital of the Inca Empire, I caught my first glimpse of the Andes—mountains so vast and imposing they made even California's Sierra Nevada seem modest. Their jagged peaks pierced the clouds, drawing a line between earth and sky, between the seen and unseen. I pressed my hand to my medicine bag, feeling the small pouch of Ojai soil within, and whispered a prayer of gratitude—for safe passage, and for the teachings to come.

Our small group of six was met at the airport by a Quechua medicine man whose weathered face and steady gaze carried the weight of ancestral knowing. He greeted each of us with a nod, assessing not with judgment but with presence—as if discerning who among us had come as true pilgrims. When his eyes met mine, a quiet recognition passed between us, though no words were spoken.

The journey to Machu Picchu would take several days, with visits to sacred sites along the way. As our van wound through Cusco's narrow streets and into the Sacred Valley, our guide began sharing the cosmology of his people. The Quechua, like the Chumash, understood the world as alive with spirit—mountains, rivers, even stones imbued with consciousness and memory. They practiced ayni, the sacred reciprocity that holds all relationships in balance—between humans, nature, and the unseen.

I listened closely, struck by how Bear's teachings echoed across this distant land. Different languages, different landscapes—yet the essence was the same. As we traveled deeper into the Sacred Valley, past terraced hills and villages where time moved slowly, I felt myself entering a different rhythm altogether. Here, the ancient and the present weren't separate—they breathed side by side, more visible than in the hurried world I had left behind.

Our first ceremonial stop was at a site where crystal springs bubbled up from the earth. Our guide invited us to cup the water in our hands—first to drink, then to touch it gently to our foreheads and hearts, before returning it to the ground as an offering.

"Water is the blood of Pachamama, Mother Earth," he said. "When we drink, we become one with her body. When we return the water, we honor that bond."

Even as modern nations emerged, Pachamama remained a living presence—benevolent, generous, and deeply revered as the sacred spirit of the land.

As I moved through the ritual, I added my own silent prayer—linking this Andean spring to the rivers of California where Bear and I had built our sweat lodge. Water to water, mountain to mountain, tradition to tradition. I was no longer just a student of these ways—I was beginning to understand my role as a bridge between them.

That evening, as we settled into a quiet lodging in the Sacred Valley, our guide approached me privately.

"You have brought something from your mountains," he said—not as a question, but as a knowing.

I nodded, startled by his perception.

"Tomorrow, we visit the ancient temple at Ollantaytambo. There is a place there where the mountains will receive your offering—if you choose to give it."

A shiver moved through me—not fear, but affirmation. The connection I had felt between these sacred lands was real, and somehow, he sensed it too. As he turned to leave, he paused.

"You have learned from other indigenous teachers. This is good. Wisdom belongs to no single people. In these times, we must share what we know, or the healing cannot spread."

His words lingered long after he walked away, leaving me to wonder: What might awaken when the soil of Ojai touched the stone of the Andes?

The ancient site of Ollantaytambo rose before us the next day, its massive stone terraces climbing the mountainside like a giant's staircase. Our guide led us through narrow passageways between walls built of stones so precisely fitted that not even a credit card could slide between them. As we climbed higher, the modern town below grew smaller, and the presence of the Inca builders seemed to grow stronger—as if time were thinning out, allowing their energy to reach across centuries.

At the summit, our guide directed the group to explore the main temple complex while beckoning me to follow him to a more secluded area. We approached what appeared to be an altar stone, worn smooth by centuries of offerings and prayers.

"Here," the guide's voice barely rose above the mountain wind as he gestured to the stone.

I removed my medicine bag and carefully unwrapped the soil from Ojai. As I placed it on the altar stone, I spoke a prayer that connected the mountains of my birth with these ancient peaks, acknowledging their kinship and asking for healing of the wounds both peoples had endured. The Quechua guide nodded in approval, offering his own whispered prayers in his native tongue.

"The mountains remember," he said afterward. "They will carry these prayers."

In the days that followed, we journeyed deeper into the sacred geography of the Andes. Each site revealed another layer of Quechua cosmology and practice. Then came the day we visited Lake Titicaca, the highest navigable lake in the world, straddling the border between Peru and Bolivia. Its vastness was breathtaking—its still water reflecting the immense blue of the Andean sky.

While the rest of our small group decided to hike to a viewpoint, I asked our guide if I might remain at the lake's edge to pray. He seemed to understand my need for solitude and nodded, pointing to a secluded spot where tall reeds lined the shore.

"The lake is sacred," he said before leaving. "It is said to be the birthplace of the Inca civilization. The waters hold great power."

Left alone, I made my way through the high reeds to the water's edge. The lake stretched before me, vast, deep and still beneath the open sky. I decided to offer my prayers from within the water itself, feeling called to make a more direct connection with this sacred place. I stepped carefully into the shallows, expecting the usual buoyancy of water to support me.

To my shock, I immediately sank, as if the water had no substance. I had to struggle back to the surface, involuntarily swallowing some of the lake water in my surprise. Its taste was unexpectedly sweet—sweeter than any natural water I had ever encountered. As I broke the surface, gasping, I noticed a young boy standing at the shore watching me with serious, intent eyes.

He appeared to be about eleven or twelve, barefoot, shirtless, and wearing only shorts despite the high-altitude chill. His presence startled me—we were in an extremely remote area, with no villages visible nearby. I had no idea where he could have come from or how he had approached so silently.

As I steadied myself in the shallows and began my prayers, the boy remained, his watchful gaze never leaving me. There was something protective in his stance, as if he were standing guard. I continued my ceremony, offering prayers to the water spirits and to Pachamama, feeling the boy's presence as a benevolent witness rather than an intrusion.

When I finished my prayers and waded back to shore, I intended to speak with him, perhaps offer him something from my pack. But in the moment it took me to gather my belongings, he vanished. I scanned the shore in all directions, but the vast open landscape offered no place for him to hide. My friends returned shortly after, and when I mentioned the boy, they looked at me curiously—they had seen no one on their hike, no villages, no signs of habitation.

A profound sense of having been witnessed by something beyond the ordinary settled over me. The boy's protective presence had felt both ancient and timeless, as if the lake itself had sent a guardian to watch over my prayers. I couldn't shake the feeling that I had been blessed by something sacred—that my intentions had been seen, understood, and honored by forces I was only beginning to comprehend.

That night, when I described the boy to our guide, a look of recognition crossed his face. "The lake has guardians," was all he said, leaving me to ponder the meaning of my encounter.

Still carrying the presence of the lake and the memory of the guardian boy, I felt the journey gathering toward its highest point. The culmination of our journey was, of course, Machu Picchu itself. We arrived early in the morning, when mist still clung to the stone structures and terraces of this city in the clouds. While others gasped at the iconic view of the ruins with Huayna Picchu rising behind them, I felt something more visceral—a magnetic pull toward the mountain peak that dominated the site.

"I need to climb Huayna Picchu," I told our guide, pointing to the steep, almost vertical mountain that overlooked the ancient city.

"It's a difficult climb," he cautioned. "Narrow trails, steep drops. It takes most people over an hour to reach the top."

I carried prayers for my brother who had passed—prayers I somehow knew belonged at the summit of this sacred mountain. To everyone's surprise, including my own, I found myself running up the ancient trail—a narrow path with rough stone steps that had been carved into the mountain over 700 years ago. The altitude was punishing, with Huayna Picchu standing at 8,924 feet above sea level, but my body moved as if pulled upward by an unseen force. What should have been an exhausting, hour-long climb became a euphoric ascent that took less than thirty minutes.

At the summit, breathless not from exertion but from awe, I lay down on my back, gazing up at the fluffy white clouds drifting across the vast Andean sky. In that moment, I felt my brother's presence with absolute clarity—as if the veil between worlds had thinned at this height, this sacred place. I spoke to him, knowing he could hear me, and left offerings of tobacco, sage, and one of my treasured owl feathers among the stones at the peak.

The descent was slower, deliberate, as I took in the breathtaking views of Machu Picchu below—this perfect integration of human creation and natural landscape, ancient stones seamlessly continuing the mountain's own contours. I understood then why the Inca were such master builders—they weren't imposing their will on the landscape but rather extending it, collaborating with the mountain's own design.

Later that day, while exploring the Temple of the Moon, I was drawn not to the main cave that attracted most visitors, but to a small stone building set slightly apart. Inside, the walls were lined with small niches, each containing a stone. Following an intuitive impulse, I began touching each stone with my hands as I walked around the interior. When I reached one particular stone, I froze, electricity seeming to course through my fingertips. The energy pulsating from this ordinary-looking rock was unlike anything I had ever experienced—a vibration so powerful it momentarily stopped my breath. What did I receive from that stone? Not words or images, but something older than language—a cellular knowing, as if the earth had whispered directly into my bones, recalibrating my understanding of what it means to communicate with the more-than-human world.

I stood there, hand connected to the stone, for what felt like both seconds and hours, receiving something I couldn't name but knew was changing me at a fundamental level. This stone, I later learned, was believed to be one of the many awakening stones or "speaking stones" of the Inca—repositories of knowledge and energy that could be accessed by those sensitive enough to receive their transmissions.

As the day drew to a close and tourists began to leave the site before the gates closed, a wild idea took hold of me. I wanted—needed—to spend the night among these sacred ruins, alone under the stars as the Inca priests might have done centuries ago. This wasn't permitted, of course; guards patrolled the grounds to ensure all visitors departed.

I told my friend I'd been inspired to stay and not to worry about me —I would meet them the next morning. Then I searched for a hiding place, finding a small cave among the ruins just large enough for me to squeeze into. From this shelter, I watched as guards with flashlights made their final sweeps of the grounds.

As darkness fell completely, I prepared to emerge from my hiding place and find a more comfortable spot to spend the night. Suddenly, a strange crackling sound just above my left ear caught my attention. I turned my small flashlight toward the noise and found myself face-to-face with two enormous spiders—each as large as the palm of my hand. Their presence quickly convinced me that the cave would not be my resting place for the night!

Carefully checking that my poncho and hat were free of eight-legged hitchhikers, I emerged into the star-filled night. Standing alone among the silent ruins, I was overcome by the realization that I was experiencing Machu Picchu as few modern people ever had—in solitude, at night, with only the stars and stones as companions. The energy of the place was entirely different now—more present, more palpable, as if the absence of crowds had allowed the true spirit of Machu Picchu to emerge from hiding.

I found a large, flat stone and lay down upon it, gazing up at stars so brilliant and numerous they seemed to form a luminous river across the sky. The stone still held the day's warmth, cradling me as I contemplated the generations of Inca who had walked these same paths, observed these same stars, and communed with these same mountains. I felt not like an intruder but like an invited guest, permitted to glimpse the true face of this sacred site.

Throughout the night, I drifted between sleep and wakefulness, dreams and visions blending with the physical reality around me. At times, I could almost hear the sounds of an ancient city alive with activity—voices speaking in Quechua, the shuffle of sandaled feet on stone, the distant notes of flutes. These sensory impressions came not as hallucinations but as memories—as if the stones themselves were sharing what they had witnessed.

When dawn began to lighten the eastern sky, I sat up to watch the sun rise over Huayna Picchu. Wild llamas and alpacas grazed peacefully nearby, unconcerned by my presence. As the first golden light touched the ancient stones, I noticed a woman sitting about a hundred meters up the hill behind me. She sat perfectly still, also watching the sunrise, her silhouette dark against the lightening sky.

After offering my morning prayers in gratitude for this extraordinary night, I stood and walked toward her. Without exchanging a single word, I placed in her hand a crystal I had been holding throughout the dawn meditation. Something in her eyes told me she understood the significance of this gift—not its material value but the energy it had absorbed during this sacred time and place. I then turned and walked away to meet my friends at the entrance, carrying with me an experience that had fundamentally shifted something in my understanding of time, space, and the thin boundaries between worlds.

As my time in Peru drew to a close, I felt there was still something incomplete—a deeper layer of connection I had yet to experience. Throughout our journey, I had witnessed the reverence the Quechua people held for their ancestral ceremonies, and I found myself drawn to ask our guide if I might be permitted to participate in one of these sacred traditions. When I made the request to our guide, he had looked at me as if I had two heads.

"Most natives do not even participate in these ceremonies," he said with surprise, "let alone a tourist!"

I met his gaze directly and replied with quiet certainty, "I am no tourist."

Something in my response must have convinced him, for the next morning before sunrise, there was a knock at my door. He motioned for me to follow without explanation. Quickly gathering my medicine bag with tobacco, sage, and feathers, I joined him as he led me to his jeep.

We drove along treacherous mountain roads until the vehicle could go no further, then continued on foot to a remote village where even the first light of dawn had not yet reached. My guide knocked on the door of a small house, which was opened by an elderly woman of diminutive stature. They conversed in Quechua for several minutes while I waited respectfully, unable to understand their words but sensing the gravity of the exchange.

Eventually, two men arrived, exchanging nods with my guide. We were led to a back building—a small room with no windows, illuminated only by oil lamps. The space was arranged with wooden pews like a church and featured a small altar adorned with feathers, stones, and colorful cloth.

I was instructed to sit as the two men prepared for the ceremony. They began singing in Quechua, their voices rising and falling in patterns utterly foreign yet somehow familiar to my ears. What appeared to be blessed water was sprinkled around the room, and then, without warning, the lamps were extinguished, plunging us into complete darkness.

What followed defies adequate description in words. As the prayers continued in the darkness, the room filled with scents of sage and herbs I couldn't identify. Then came the unmistakable sensation of presences entering the space—spirits of the mountains, as I would later learn, along with the unmistakable sound of great wings moving through the air around us. These were the spirits of the condor, sacred bird of the Andes, whose wingspan can reach over ten feet.

For several hours, we sat in that darkness as the invisible world became tangible, audible, present in ways that transcended normal sensory experience. The ceremony was not performed for my benefit or entertainment—I was simply permitted to witness an ancient communion between the Quechua people and the spirits with whom they had been in relationship for thousands of years.

When at last the lamps were relit, I blinked in the sudden light, feeling as if I had returned from a journey to another dimension. In gratitude, I offered the shaman tobacco, sage, and several of my owl feathers. He accepted them with dignity and, to my surprise, presented me with a single condor feather in return.

"This is for healing," he explained through my guide. "It carries the spirit of the mountains and the sky. Use it with respect when you return home."

That feather became one of my most sacred possessions—a tangible connection to the extraordinary experiences I had been privileged to receive in Peru. It was a reminder of the bridge I had helped to build between indigenous healing traditions—separated by vast distances yet connected in their reverence for the sacred.

As my plane lifted off from Cusco days later, I looked down at the Andes receding below me, knowing I was leaving with far more than photographs and souvenirs. I carried new dimensions of healing knowledge, connections between traditions, and a deeper understanding of how ancient wisdom still whispers to those willing to listen—across continents, across time, and transcending the constructed limits that seem to separate us from each other and the earth.

The Andean whisper had become part of my own breath now, joining with the teachings of Bear, the heritage of the Chumash, and my own evolving path as a healer. These traditions, I understand now, are not separate streams but tributaries of the same great river—still flowing for those with the ears to hear, the heart to listen, and the courage to step in.

Back home, I discovered how profoundly these experiences had changed my healing practice. The mountain spirits and ancient wisdoms had woven themselves into my work. The condor feather became a bridge between worlds during sessions, the speaking stone's cellular knowing guided my hands in ways I'm still learning to understand, and the guardian boy's protective presence reminds me that we are never alone in our service to healing. The Andean whisper continues to inform every prayer, every ceremony, every moment I hold space for others' healing journeys—proof that wisdom shared across cultures multiplies rather than diminishes, creating a web of healing that spans both geography and time.

INVITATION TO PAUSE

- Have you ever felt the presence of the land as more than landscape—alive, listening, guiding? What does it mean to you to be in relationship with the more-than-human world?
- Consider looking at a tree, a stone, a bird, a cloud—just look, without naming it. What do you notice? What does this wordless seeing awaken in you?
- Where in your life do you sense the presence of guardians or guides—seen or unseen—who watch over your spiritual journey?
- Be quiet. Observe, notice. Allow spaciousness to rise—not as thought, but as relationship, as reverence, as belonging. Feel the earth beneath you. Breathe as One.

THE WAY OF HARMONY

"Peace is not something we impose—
it's what arises when we dissolve the conflict within."

There are universal principles that flow through all aspects of my life—
martial arts, healing, spiritual mediumship, and everyday interaction.
These principles transcend their specific applications, revealing themselves as facets of a singular truth: that harmony arises through connection, not domination; through acceptance, not resistance. Just as in
Aikido, I learn to blend with energy rather than resist it. In my practice
of mediumship, I've found that the same principles create clarity across
the veil—through receiving rather than forcing, through allowing
instead of controlling. As you read this story, even if you've never
stepped onto a martial arts mat, I invite you to recognize how these principles of presence, awareness, receptivity, and compassionate response
might weave into your own life. For in the end, whether we are moving
through forms, holding space for another's healing, or navigating rela-

tionships, the fundamental principles remain the same when rooted in love.

HOME OF AIKIDO

The cherry blossoms had not yet awakened when I arrived in Tokyo that spring of 2009. The air held a crisp promise of renewal as I made my way through the crowded streets, carrying my well-worn travel bag containing little more than my training uniform—a white keikogi and black hakama that had journeyed with me to dojos across America for decades. At forty-seven, I had been practicing Aikido for nearly thirty years, the art had become as essential to me as breath. For ten of those years, I had been teaching at the university, guiding students through the very transformative movements that had shaped my sense of harmony, balance, and presence.

My dojo in California, Shinzen Dojo, had been affiliated with the Pacific Aikido Federation since 2002, an organization that maintains direct lineage to the Aikido World Headquarters in Tokyo. This connection wasn't merely organizational—it represented an unbroken transmission of wisdom from the founder, Morihei Ueshiba, through generations of teachers who understood Aikido not as mere physical technique, but as a path to spiritual awakening.

Standing before Hombu Dojo in Tokyo's Wakamatsu-cho, I felt the weight of history and the lightness of anticipation. This headquarters of the Aikikai Foundation—more than a building—was the source from which the art of peace had flowed into the world.

My journey was one of *shugyō*—an intensive training that transcends technique and cultivates self-awareness. In the tradition taught through the Pacific Aikido Federation, we understood that the true purpose of training wasn't simply to master techniques, but to return to one's true self, allowing the principles of Aikido to infuse every aspect of daily life. The founder was clear: "True victory is victory over oneself." Not over an opponent, not over another—but over the reactive patterns and limitations of one's own mind.

The five-story dojo hummed with constant activity, the rhythmic sounds of feet on tatami mats and the crisp snap of uniforms composing a symphony of dedicated practice. Training sessions began at 6:30 a.m. and continued until evening, with practitioners from every corner of the world moving in and out throughout the day. Here, nationality, language, and background dissolved in shared practice—a universal language that needed no translation.

On my first morning, I arrived before dawn. Even after decades of training, my heart beat with both anticipation and exhilaration. This was a lifelong dream: to train at Aikido's home dojo in Japan. I bowed at the threshold and slipped off my shoes. The wooden floors gleamed, worn smooth by years of bare feet tracing the same path. In the changing room, I nodded to the other early risers—two Australians, a Japanese woman, and others—each silently preparing for class. Donning the same white and black uniform, I was reminded that on the mat, we weren't defined by worldly identities, but by the sincerity of our practice.

I had come to train with Moriteru Ueshiba Doshu, the third Doshu (hereditary head) of Aikido and grandson of the founder. Each morning at 6:30 a.m., he led the first class of the day. Stepping onto the tatami, I felt a living link to every teacher in my lineage who had walked this path before me. He entered with quiet grace and precision, bowing toward the shomen—the front of the dojo where a photograph of the founder hung beside calligraphy expressing the art's principles. We bowed in turn —first to the *shōmen*, then to the Doshu—before beginning the familiar warm-up movements of Aikido. What struck me immediately was the depth of silence—not the absence of sound, but a collected stillness of mind. Breath, movement, and the occasional word of instruction filled the room, yet beneath it all was a shared stillness—a collective discipline of focused awareness.

One morning, a moment unfolded that would become one of the most memorable of my journey. My training partner had stepped briefly off the mat, and I sat in *seiza*—the formal kneeling position—awaiting his return. To my surprise, Doshu approached and asked, in simple English,

"Where did your partner go?"

"He just stepped off the mat for a moment," I replied, doing my best to stay composed despite my racing heart.

Doshu bowed to me—a gesture that carried the weight of generations—and asked if I would practice with him. The invitation was so unexpected and I bowed in silent gratitude.

As we moved, his touch gentle—strength without force, no strain, no hint of imposed will. I felt wholly supported, as I was redirected, and falling felt more like flying. That brief exchange stayed with me as a powerful reminder—a practice of presence, a way of being rather than doing.

Days at Hombu Dojo settled into a rhythm: early morning training with the Doshu, breakfast at a small local café—where the owner soon came to recognize me and had my tea ready—afternoon sessions with senior instructors, and evening practice before returning to my small rented room. I fell asleep deeply each night, muscles pleasantly fatigued, my mind quieted by hours of training.

But Tokyo was only the beginning of my pilgrimage. After two weeks immersed in the intensity of Hombu Dojo, I prepared to journey to more remote parts of Japan, seeking out teachers who had received the founder's direct transmission—living embodiments of Aikido's origin.

THE ALL-JAPAN AIKIDO DEMONSTRATION

The 47th All-Japan Aikido Demonstration at the Tokyo Budokan marked a turning point in my journey. This annual gathering brings together thousands of Aikido practitioners from across Japan and around the world to demonstrate the depth and diversity of the art. I arrived early, finding a seat in the stands of the massive arena, camera in hand, ready to capture the experience for my students back home.

Row upon row of pristine white uniforms filled the floor of the

Budokan, the black *hakama* adding a visual rhythm as practitioners moved through synchronized warm-ups. The energy in the building was palpable—a blend of reverence and celebration befitting such a gathering of devoted practitioners.

I was content to observe from the stands—until something unexpected changed everything. A young Japanese man made his way up the steps, scanning faces until his eyes met mine. He approached and bowed low.

"Excuse me," he said in careful English. "Are you an Aikido teacher visiting from America?"

When I confirmed this, his face lit up. "Kubota Sensei sent me to find you. He would be honored if you would join our dojo's demonstration."

Without hesitation, he bowed again and handed me his neatly folded uniform—offering it so I could take my place with their group. His gesture spoke volumes: a quiet act of humility and respect, embodying the very principles we practiced on the mat.

The invitation caught me completely by surprise. Ikuhiro Kubota Shihan, an 8th-degree black belt and founder of the Nara Aikikai, was one of the teachers I had trained with in the U.S. when he visited years earlier. That he had recognized me among thousands and extended this invitation felt profound, if not miraculous.

"It would be my honor," I said, quickly gathering my things.

Minutes later, we bowed to each other on the floor of the Budokan —an unexpected reunion forged not through words, but through shared practice and mutual respect.

The members of Nara Aikikai greeted me with warm smiles and respectful bows, welcoming me into their formation as though I had always belonged. In that moment, I felt the true essence of Aikido: an unforced invitation rooted in mutual respect and shared presence.

As we waited in the hallway for our turn to demonstrate, my hands trembled slightly, and my heart quickened. The thought of thousands of eyes watching—including Doshu himself—brought a rush of anticipation. I was grateful for the spontaneity—had I known days in advance, the pressure might have been overwhelming.

When our group stepped onto the floor, we began with synchronized warm-ups, then transitioned into basic techniques and then more advanced exchanges. I was paired with one of the senior students, and though we had never practiced together, our movements flowed with effortless harmony. This was the quiet miracle of Aikido—a shared language of presence that transcended words.

Later, when I thanked Kubota Sensei for including me, he smiled and said, "In Aikido, there are no strangers, only family we've yet to meet." His words echoed something I had long felt: Aikido offers more than movement. It offers a way of meeting the world—with openness, dignity, and peace.

From Tokyo, my journey continued to the ancient city of Nara, where I spent a week in daily training at Kubota Sensei's dojo. The contrast between the bustling energy of Hombu Dojo and the quiet focus of this traditional space was striking. Here, training was interspersed with philosophical conversations over green tea, walks through temple grounds, and moments of quiet reflection that felt as essential to the practice as the physical techniques themselves.

Kubota Sensei embodied the integration of Aikido principles into daily life. Whether demonstrating a complex pin on the mat or gently arranging flowers in the small alcove of the dojo, the same quality of focused presence infused his every movement. "Aikido is not something we do," he told me one evening as we sat in his small garden. "It is something we become."

HEART OF GRATITUDE—HEART OF LOVE

The next phase of my pilgrimage took me deeper into Japan, to the Kumano region of Wakayama Prefecture. This area, known for its sacred pilgrimage routes and ancient shrines hidden in forested mountains, felt like stepping into another world—where the veil between the physical and spiritual realms seemed especially thin.

It was here that I sought out Motomichi Anno Sensei, an 8th-degree black belt and direct student of the founder, Morihei Ueshiba. He was renowned for his profound understanding of Aikido's spiritual dimensions—elements the founder emphasized, but which are often diluted in modern practice.

Anno Sensei's dojo—the Kumano Juku Dojo in Shingu—was modest in size, yet rich in spirit. Nestled in a region long regarded as Japan's spiritual heart, the dojo radiated a quiet energy that touched everyone who entered. Training here felt different—movements emerged not from deliberate thought, but from a deep attunement to something greater.

"Aikido is a matter of the heart—a heart of gratitude," Anno Sensei said during one session, his voice gentle yet penetrating. "Aikido is, ultimately, about Love." His words echoed O-Sensei's own teachings: that the heart of Aikido lies in continuous self-purification and reflection—where true victory is not over another, but over oneself. Anno Sensei explained, "We continue training to purify the heart and reveal the light of Love within—cultivating harmony, gratitude, and compassion."

During my time with Anno Sensei, he took me to visit Nachi Falls —Japan's tallest waterfall—tucked within a sacred primeval forest. We hiked together beneath towering trees, their ancient roots twisting across the path like living guardians of old wisdom. A young woman accompanied us as an interpreter, since Anno Sensei spoke primarily in Japanese.

As we made our way toward the falls, I noticed something remarkable unfolding. The young interpreter became so absorbed in Anno Sensei's teachings that she occasionally forgot to translate. Rather than feeling disconnected, I found myself attuning to the sound and vibration of his words. To my surprise, I understood—not through language, but through a deeper, intuitive transmission. He was speaking about Aikido as a matter of the heart, explaining that at its essence, it is Love.

This experience of intuitive understanding deepened during another profound moment at his dojo. Anno Sensei called me into his office, where he knelt in seiza with a small table between us. I knelt as well, one of his senior students positioned slightly behind me. Anno Sensei began reading from handwritten pages, speaking in Japanese without pausing for translation. For a moment, I wondered if he realized I couldn't understand the words—but then something shifted. As I settled into the rhythm and resonance of his voice, the meaning flowed into my heart—comprehension bypassing language, transmitted soul to soul.

One afternoon, after an especially intense training session, Anno Sensei invited me for a walk to a shrine deep within the forest. We walked in silence along an ancient path, lined with moss-covered stone lanterns and 538 steep steps that led to the top of a small hill above the city. The only sounds were our breath, our footsteps, and the occasional call of a bird hidden among the trees.

At the summit, a small shrine sat just beneath a massive boulder, overlooking the city of Shingu and the Pacific Ocean. Anno Sensei explained that each year, a fire festival takes place at the shrine, where participants run from the top to the bottom carrying torches. As we sat together, quietly taking in the view, Anno Sensei spoke of the founder's vision.

"O-Sensei saw Aikido as a gift for healing a broken world," he said. "Not as a set of techniques, but as a path to remember our fundamental connection to all things. When he spoke of harmony, he meant not just harmony between two people on the mat, but harmony with the universe itself."

In that moment, surrounded by the ancient forest of Kumano, a deeper understanding took root—not intellectual, but embodied. Aikido was not separate from my healing work, my studies in psychology, or my explorations of indigenous wisdom. They were all facets of the same essential inquiry: how to live in right relationship—with ourselves, each other, and with the great mystery that holds us all.

As my time with Anno Sensei drew to a close, he invited me to his office one final time. There, with the same heart-filled care he brought to every aspect of his practice, he presented me with a gift—a scroll of his own calligraphy, created specifically for my dojo in California. The bold, flowing strokes embodied the same essence I had witnessed in his Aikido —love and gratitude in perfect balance.

"This is for your students," he said through an interpreter, though I felt I understood his intention directly. The calligraphy depicted characters representing harmony, spirit, and the path—each reflecting O-Sensei's vision for Aikido as a practice to help heal the world's discord by beginning within.

This gift represented more than a souvenir or memento. It was a living link between his dojo and mine, between the teachings I had received in Japan and those I would carry forward with my students. This calligraphy would serve as a bridge between sacred spaces, transmitting both energy and intention across oceans.

As I carefully wrapped the scroll for the journey home, I felt the quiet weight of responsibility that comes with such a transmission. The teachings I had received were not mine to keep, but to carry forward— preserving their essence while allowing them to find new expression through my own deepening understanding, my continued self-purification, and the practice of a heart rooted in Love and gratitude.

A FEARLESS HEART

My journey through Japan continued to Hiroshi Tada Sensei's dojo in Jiyugaoka, Tokyo. A 9th-degree black belt, Tada Sensei was among the highest-ranked Aikido teachers in the world and, like Anno Sensei, had received direct instruction from the founder. Though in his mid-eighties at the time of my visit, he moved with the lightness and precision of someone decades younger.

His teaching style was both demanding and compassionate— requiring absolute commitment, while honoring each student's path. "In Aikido," he told me during one training session, "we do not aim for perfection of technique but for perfection of character through technique."

This emphasis on Aikido as a path of moral and spiritual growth, rather than merely physical training, was consistent across all the teachers I sought out in Japan—each expressing it through their own unique perspective. While Anno Sensei emphasized attunement to subtle energy and the heart of gratitude and love, Tada Sensei focused on cultivating what he called a "fearless heart"—not the absence of fear, but the capacity to move forward with integrity in its presence.

"The mat is a mirror," he said one evening after training, as we gathered around him. "It shows us not who we wish to be, but who we are now. Our work is to meet that reflection with honesty and compassion."

RETURN TO HOMBU AND INTEGRATION

As my two months in Japan neared their conclusion, I returned to Hombu Dojo in Tokyo for the final week of my pilgrimage. The circular nature of the journey felt fitting—ending where it had begun, yet carrying within me the teachings and experiences gathered along the way.

The morning class on my final day was taught by Moriteru Ueshiba Doshu. As we moved through the familiar forms, I felt a sense of wholeness—the heart of love from Anno Sensei, the emphasis on character from Tada Sensei, and the familial spirit of Kubota Sensei—all present in the simple act of receiving a partner's attack and transforming it into harmony.

After class, I approached the Doshu to express my gratitude for the opportunity to train at Hombu Dojo. He smiled warmly and asked about my experiences in Japan. When I mentioned the teachers I had sought out, his eyes lit with recognition. "You have received many gifts," he said with quiet certainty. "Now your responsibility is to carry them forward and transmit them faithfully."

THE FIVE SPIRITS OF BUDO EMBODIED

As I reflected on my journey throughout Japan, I began to recognize how the traditional principles of Budo had manifested in my experiences with each teacher. These weren't abstract concepts but living transmissions, passed on through direct experience. Each had transmitted these not as theory, but as lived reality.

The five fundamental spirits of Budo began to reveal themselves—not merely as concepts, but as embodied truths. These principles, long present in my Aikido training, now resonated with a clarity that felt both familiar and new.

Shoshin—beginner's mind—became more than a training concept; it was the lens through which I navigated Japan itself. Despite my decades of practice, I approached each dojo with the fresh openness of a new student, ready to "steal the techniques" as O-Sensei had instructed. At Hombu Dojo, watching senior practitioners in their seventies and eighties still training with the eager attention of beginners reminded me that true mastery isn't an endpoint but a continual openness to discovery.

One quiet morning at Kubota Sensei's dojo, he shifted my stance with a small adjustment to my foot—a reminder that refinement never ends. "Even after fifty years," he said with a soft smile, "I still find new understanding in *tenkan* (turning)." In that moment, I saw *Shoshin* not as a beginner's mindset but as a master's secret—the doorway through which wisdom continues to enter.

Zanshin—lingering mind—revealed itself most powerfully during the All Japan Aikido Demonstration. As thousands of practitioners filled the *Budokan*, I witnessed how the best demonstrations maintained an unbroken connection beyond the execution of technique. This wasn't merely awareness—it was a sustained attunement of spirit that endured in the spaces between form, transcending the boundaries of physical expression.

When practicing with Tada Sensei, I noticed how his attention stayed with me even after a technique ended. His presence didn't break; it simply continued. "Aikido happens in the spaces between techniques," he said, "not just during the obvious movements." This quality of *Zanshin*—a steady presence that held the partner, the space, and the moment—began to infuse my awareness both on and off the mat.

Mushin—no mind—was perhaps the most elusive spirit, yet Japan created the perfect conditions for its emergence. During an intensive training session with Anno Sensei, as the dojo filled with twenty practitioners moving in a continuous flow of attack and response, I experienced a moment where my analytical mind completely ceased. Without warning, time seemed to expand infinitely, and I found myself responding to attacks with fluidity, moving without thinking, responding without planning. The techniques emerged from somewhere deeper than conscious thought, as if my body remembered what my mind had forgotten. Anno Sensei noticed the shift and nodded slightly, a wordless acknowledgment that I had glimpsed, the state where technique and practitioner become one. When the mind is still, there are endless possibilities. This taste of *mushin*—this brief liberation from the constraints of thinking—revealed the paradox at Aikido's heart: we train diligently to ultimately transcend training itself.

Fudoshin—immovable mind—was not about physical rigidity, but about cultivating an unshakable center amid constant change. This quality was embodied by all the great teachers I encountered. One evening after training, an elderly Japanese practitioner who had studied directly with the founder shared his insight with me. "The mountain does not resist the wind," he said. "It remains the mountain. This is *fudoshin*." I began to understand that true immovability comes not from bracing against life's challenges but from being so deeply rooted in one's center that no external force can truly unsettle it.

Senshin—purified spirit or enlightened attitude—felt like the natural culmination of the other four spirits. I glimpsed it throughout my journey: in a teacher's gentle correction, in the quiet support between partners, and in the way Anno Sensei treated everyone—from senior practitioners to the cleaning staff—with equal care and presence.

One rainy afternoon at a small mountain dojo near Kyoto, I watched a teacher in his nineties move with such grace that his Aikido felt more like a blessing than a technique. After class, speaking through an interpreter, he said, "For seventy years I trained to defeat attackers. Now I understand—I train to reconcile conflict in the universe. This is O-Sensei's gift to us."

These five spirits were not separate teachings but interwoven expressions of a single path. *Shoshin* allowed me to see with fresh eyes, *zanshin* kept me connected to each experience, *mushin* freed me from interfering thoughts, *fudoshin* provided stability amid intensity, and *senshin* pointed toward the deeper purpose of training—a harmonizing spirit that might, in some small way, help restore balance to a fractured world.

As I moved through Japan, these principles began to merge with my understanding of healing work. The same qualities that shape transformative Aikido—present attention, unbroken connection, freedom from preconceptions, stable presence, and compassionate intention—also shaped transformative healing. The path of Aikido and the path of healing were not separate journeys, but reflections of the same awakening.

Today, these five spirits have found new expression in my work as a medium. *Shoshin* allows me to approach each session with fresh openness and no preconceptions about what might come through. *Zanshin* helps me stay connected with both client and spirit, while *Mushin* offers the clear, still pond where messages arise without distortion. *Fudoshin* offers the grounded stability that allows me to stay centered, even when difficult or emotional messages arise. And *Senshin* guides the ultimate purpose of this work—not merely to affirm the continuity of consciousness, but to heal relationships and foster reconciliation across the veil.

What Japan taught me, in essence, was that Aikido is not ultimately about self-defense or even physical movement—it is about harmonizing energy, transmuting conflict into connection, and becoming a clear channel through which healing can flow. Whether on the mat, in a healing session, or while serving as a medium, the principles remain the same: release ego, trust the process, stay present, and allow divine love to move through you freely and without resistance.

As my pilgrimage drew to a close, I reflected on how these timeless principles would continue to shape my path forward long after leaving Japan.

THE PATH CONTINUES

As I prepared to leave, I realized my time in Japan had deepened my understanding not just of Aikido techniques but of Aikido as a spiritual path—one that offered profound insights into the nature of conflict, harmony, and transformation. What I had embodied through decades of practice on the mat now guided my service as a healer and medium: receiving energy with openness, choosing harmony over force, and honoring the sacred thread within each exchange.

The founder of Aikido, Morihei Ueshiba, had often spoken of his art as *misogi*—a practice of purification that could help cleanse the world of discord and disharmony. My time in Japan had deepeded my understanding—that by transforming our relationship with conflict, we might contribute to its transformation on a larger scale.

On my final evening in Tokyo, I visited a small Shinto shrine near my lodging. As dusk settled over the city, I sat in meditation, offering gratitude for the journey and all it had revealed. A gentle rain began to fall—cleansing water from the sky meeting earth in quiet unity, a natural harmony beyond words or technique.

In that moment, I understood something essential about both Aikido and healing: that our most profound work is not to create harmony where it does not exist, but to attune to the harmony that already exists in all things. Our practice—whether on the mat or in life—is simply to remove the obstacles that prevent us from experiencing this truth directly.

As I boarded the plane home, my body still carrying the muscle memory of countless repetitions, I realized the pilgrimage's true gift wasn't sharper technique but the deepening of perception—the ability to perceive more clearly the patterns of connection that bind us to one another and to the greater whole.

In the end, whether practicing Aikido, offering healing, or simply moving through the world with awareness, the essential practice remains the same: to harmonize with what is, to move with rather than against the currents of life, and to transform conflict into connection through the alchemy of presence and compassion. And in this harmony, we discover O-Sensei's deepest teaching—that true victory is not about winning over others, but transcending the discord within our own minds.

INVITATION TO PAUSE

- Consider someone in your life you may struggle to understand—perhaps someone with whom you disagree, or whose actions confuse or upset you.
- Now, for just a moment, imagine standing in their shoes. Feel the weight of their life—their longings, fears, wounds, and hopes. What might they be carrying that you cannot see?
- Breathe into this imagining. Let your breath soften the edges of resistance. Feel into their perspective, not to agree, but to understand.
- How does your heart respond when you step out of judgment and into empathy? What shifts inside you when you see through their eyes, even for a breath?
- Pause. Let that spaciousness widen. In this quiet stillness, what truth do you feel?

THE HEALING LIGHT WITHIN

"What you seek has always been within.
The practice is simply to turn your attention."

In the autumn of 2019, life shifted beneath me with a single, decisive moment. A car accident—minor by outward measure—turned my head just so, a twist too far. I thought I was ok at first, but the next day the pain flared, sharp and unyielding, radiating from my neck into my spine like lightning. Weeks later, the doctor's words fell heavy: one step from quadriplegia, a bump away from a wheelchair.

Nerve pain shot into my feet, and nights stretched endlessly as I paced, tracing the ache's relentless dance. Yet within that crucible of suffering, something deeper stirred—a whisper of surrender, a call to stillness I had learned to recognize. I had faced shadows before: grief's crushing weight, fear's sharp edge. But this pain was different—a test of both flesh and spirit that demanded everything I had learned about healing.

Where once I had moved with fluid grace through Aikido forms, now simply turning my head became a monumental challenge. The physical limitation felt like a cruel joke—the very practices that had taught me about flow and non-resistance now seemed beyond my reach. Doctors warned me, absolutely no more martial arts training. Yet perhaps this was the ultimate lesson: to find that flow not in external movement, but in the deepest chambers of my being.

I turned inward, observing the pain as it ebbed and surged like an ocean tide—a rhythm I could neither control nor escape. Each breath became a prayer, a practice of presence, meeting the fire with whatever grace I could summon. The pain was relentless, demanding my full attention day and night. I could feel my body's instinct to fight, to resist, to rage against this unwelcome visitor.

Fear rose like dark water as I imagined this might never change—or worse, might progress as the neurosurgeon predicted. In those moments when fear threatened to overwhelm me, my inner teacher stepped forward with familiar wisdom: "Bring yourself back to center as you have practiced. Focus attention on the breath. Observe, don't resist."

In that mindful practice, I began to notice something profound: pain changes. It is never fixed, never permanent, despite how it feels in the moment. And in its very flux, I found an unexpected gift—stillness. Not the absence of sensation, but a deeper peace that could hold it all. I practiced not to resist but to flow with it, trusting love's quiet power to guide me through.

Days blurred into weeks, months, then two years. I paced when sleep eluded me, sharp currents shooting through my feet, yet I held fast to that inner gaze. The question that had carried me through my brother's passing and moments of fear in France returned to anchor me: "Could I surrender this too?"

There were moments when doubt crept in like evening shadows. "What if this is permanent?" my mind would whisper in the darkest hours before dawn. Yet even as fear arose, I practiced watching it too—not as truth, but as another visitor passing through the field of awareness. What we resist persists, my Aikido training had taught me, and so I learned to bow to each fear rather than battle it.

Throughout my days, I practiced seeing my cervical spine completely healed, visualizing healing light within, rebuilding damaged tissue and bone with luminous precision. Held in spirit's embrace—that constant presence I had known since childhood—I leaned into love for my body and mind, meeting all that arose in my awareness with compassion.

Love's light, I knew, waits within us all—a wellspring deeper than despair, more enduring than pain. I rested in its glow, allowing stillness to move through the storm of my experience.

The day came when I returned to my neurosurgeon to discuss surgery. To our mutual amazement, when he examined my latest scans, he marveled at what he saw—or rather, what he didn't see. Scans in hand, he shook his head in wonder: "I have never seen this in thirty years of practice as a neurosurgeon—complete healing, no trace of injury."

He pressed me with the urgency of a scientist encountering the impossible: "What did you do? I need to share this with my patients." I paused, searching for words to convey what felt beyond language, then said simply, "It's the light within—surrender is what opens the door."

Words faltered to convey it fully—not a method or technique, but a yielding, a trust in love's eternal pulse. The pain had not vanished overnight like some magic trick; it had softened, shifted, transformed until my body mirrored the peace I had cultivated within. What he called a miracle, I knew as spirit's quiet work—a gift born of releasing struggle and flowing with what is.

Perhaps you have known this too—a wound so deep it creates a space for light to enter, a surrender that heals beyond reason's grasp. For me, that accident wove together Aikido's grace, spirit's whispers, and love's fierce permanence into the very marrow of my bones.

I could not force the mending any more than I could force the sunrise. But in letting go, I found the strength that waits within us all— a wellspring that transcends body and fear, a light that no darkness can extinguish.

This experience transformed not just my spine, but my entire approach to healing and teaching. When guiding others through pain—

whether physical, emotional, or spiritual—I now know that true healing often begins when we stop fighting against what is and instead create space for transformation to arise naturally, in its own perfect time and way.

The light you seek has always been within you. The practice is simply to turn your attention toward it, to trust it, and to surrender to its healing power. In that surrender, miracles become not extraordinary events, but the natural expression of love's infinite capacity to heal and transform.

What seemed like my greatest limitation became my greatest teacher, showing me that within every wound lies a doorway to wholeness, and within every moment of surrender lies the possibility of profound healing.

Invitation to Pause

- Notice what your body and spirit are telling you right now. Are there places of tension, fatigue, or restlessness calling for your attention? How might you respond in this moment? What do you notice? Can you hold with compassion what ever arises?
- Bring gentle awareness to any discomfort—physical, emotional, or spiritual—that you're carrying. What wisdom might be waiting beneath these sensations? What would it feel like to offer no resistance and simply allow yourself to be exactly as you are right now?
- Breathe into this present moment. Can you sense a light within you—not something you need to create or earn, but something already here, revealed through surrender?

PART IV

Surrendering to Spirit

PREFACE TO PART IV

In the journey of a richly lived life, paths unfold in ways we could never predict. As the river of my experiences has flowed—through martial arts, bodywork, healing, and counseling—each practice has carried me to this unexpected shore: the sacred work of spiritual mediumship.

This final section of my memoir explores how years of discipline in the dojo, sensitivity honed through therapeutic touch, and a lifetime of spiritual practice have come together in what has become my life's most integrated work. What began as curiosity during the enforced stillness of a global pandemic blossomed into a calling that draws upon every skill, every surrender, every lesson I have ever practiced.

These chapters tell the story of discovering that my lifelong sensitivity—once framed as a weakness—was actually my greatest gift. They chronicle my journey from skeptic to student, from practitioner to vessel, as I learned to stand humbly in service between worlds. Along the way, mentors like Suzanne Giesemann, Eileen Davies, and Sally Hawk guided me into a discipline as rigorous as martial arts and as nuanced as structural integration.

The stories shared here reveal not just the evidence that has convinced me of life's continuity beyond physical death, but the profound parallels between these different practices. In mediumship as in Aikido, true power flows not from force but from surrender—a yielding to the greater flow, rooted in humility. The same principles that taught me to blend with a partner's energy now allow me to attune to the subtle vibrations of those who have crossed the veil.

"Surrendering to Spirit" explores this sacred meeting ground—where science meets spirit, where evidence meets faith, where love bridges physical separation. It is an invitation to consider that perhaps our most personal journey is also our most connected—that when we empty ourselves completely, we become vessels for something greater than ourselves.

This work has taught me that the culmination of a life's journey often appears in unexpected forms. The thread that weaves through all my practices—surrender, presence, compassion—now finds its fullest expression in creating bridges of healing across the threshold of worlds. In sharing these stories, I offer not certainty but wonder, not answers but exploration, and above all, the transformative power of surrendering into love's vast embrace.

MENTORS IN MEDIUMSHIP

*"The path I walk is illuminated by the wisdom
of those who came before me."*

The first sacred connection began with an unexpected encounter—not
with a person, but with a story. In 2018, as my bodywork practice
thrived, a documentary called *"Messages of Hope"* appeared in my online
recommendations. I clicked play, expecting perhaps a pleasant diversion.
Instead, I found myself captivated by the story of Suzanne Giesemann, a
former Navy Commander and aide to the Chairman of the Joint Chiefs
of Staff, whose rigorous military background seemed worlds away from
spiritual mediumship.

Her story resonated not because it was mystical but because it was
grounded—evidence-based, intellectually honest, and shaped by both
personal loss and scientific curiosity. Here was someone who
approached the unseen with the same dedication to integrity that I had
brought to my own healing work. Until then, mediumship had existed
at the periphery of my awareness—something associated with carnival

171

tents or television performances, not a serious spiritual practice. Through Suzanne's lens, I glimpsed something entirely different: a discipline as demanding as martial arts, as nuanced as structural integration, and as transformative as deep meditation.

When I learned she offered training workshops, curiosity compelled me forward. I attended my first session with Suzanne carrying a delicate blend of openness and discernment that had guided me throughout my life. As someone on the spiritual path since I was very young and as an established practitioner in my field, I might have approached it with the confidence of expertise. Instead, as a lifelong martial artist, I stepped in with humility and an open heart—embracing *shoshin*, or beginner's mind—setting aside what I knew to make space for what I had yet to learn.

"Evidence is essential," Suzanne emphasized during that first workshop, her voice carrying the calm authority of someone accustomed to briefing admirals. "Without it, we offer comfort but not conviction." She taught us to notice specific details—not vague impressions, but verifiable information that could not be explained by chance or generalization. She referred to these as "Gold Nuggets"—specific evidence such as a distinctive characteristic or an unusual nickname—details that could only arise from genuine connection with loved ones across the veil. This discipline resonated with my own approach to bodywork and psychotherapy, where careful observation reveals patterns invisible to casual attention.

What surprised me most was not the techniques she taught but the ethical framework she embodied. Here was mediumship not as entertainment or ego gratification, but as service—a sacred responsibility to connect those grieving with evidence of their loved ones' continued existence. The parallels to my own healing, bodywork, and counseling practice were striking. I have always seen my hands as conduits, not sources —channels for a wisdom greater than my own. This was no different in essence, only in expression.

Inspired by Suzanne's approach, I sought more training, a deeper commitment beyond weekend workshops. Research led me across the ocean to the Arthur Findlay College in England, renowned as the world's foremost institution for the study of mediumship and psychic sciences. I went for personal growth, desiring always a deeper awareness of spirit, never imagining it would become more than an exploration. Arriving at Arthur Findlay College felt like stepping into a mystical *Hogwarts*, straight from the pages of *Harry Potter*. This Gothic Revival estate, donated in 1923, had been established as a residential center dedicated to Spiritualist philosophy, spiritual healing, psychic sciences, and spiritual mediumship.

On the first night at Arthur Findlay, I discovered a welcome letter on my pillow that began, "Dear Sensitive, Welcome." The words stopped me, a catch rising in my throat. All my life, I had been told I was "too sensitive"—at home, in school, and even in professional settings. This was my first experience of sensitivity being seen not as a weakness to overcome but as a gift to cultivate. What had been framed as a flaw throughout my life was now recognized as a strength, a necessary quality for the work ahead.

Walking through the college corridors felt like coming home. Here, sensitivity—and what I had long named as intuition—was not only accepted, but expected. For nearly a century, world-renowned teachers have learned and taught in these halls: Gordon Higginson, who served as president of the Spiritualists' National Union and principal of Arthur Findlay College until 1993, and Glyn Edwards, another highly respected medium and tutor. Both were mentors to Eileen Davies, an extraordinary medium and spiritual teacher who would become my mentor.

While most students attended for two weeks, I stayed for two months—following the same deep immersion that had characterized my approach to martial arts and bodywork. Those months of immersive training became a foundation, the solid ground from which— though I didn't know it then—a new practice would grow. I took several courses with Eileen Davies, an exceptional medium who began her training at seventeen under Gordon and Glyn's guidance. With over forty-five years of professional experience, she is widely respected for her accuracy, integrity, and humility. Her loving kindness and deep trust in spirit gently nurtured my budding mediumship practice—a way of working with the unseen she embraced not with ego, but with deep reverence. What began as curiosity transformed into dedication as I studied under her guidance. Only later would I understand just how pivotal that connection would become—especially when the unthinkable happened.

COVID swept across the world in early 2020, abruptly closing the doors of my bodywork practice—three decades of work and relationships, suddenly suspended in the strange hush of lockdown. After decades of connection through touch, my hands were suddenly still. Yet in that quiet, I noticed something else: the luminous web of connection I had always sensed through my fingertips was still accessible—only now in a different form.

Rather than feeling only loss, I found myself curious—even excited—about what might emerge from this forced pause. The universe had created space in my life, and somehow I sensed this wasn't an ending but a transition. In this unforeseen space of possibility, I dove even deeper into mediumship as Eileen and other teachers in the UK transitioned their instruction online.

Since then, I have continued working with Eileen almost biweekly. It has been a great honor and privilege to learn from such an extraordinary teacher and medium. For over five years, her direct mentorship has nurtured my developing abilities and strengthened my confidence in the practice of mediumship. I believe any success I have in mediumship is due to the spirit world's guidance—and standing on the shoulders of these great teachers—Suzanne, who remains an ongoing spiritual teacher and who first showed me the evidence-based path, and Eileen, whose patient guidance continues to deepen my development with such care.

In early 2021, my mediumship practice took a significant turn when my classmate Sally Hawk invited me to participate in a prototype program that would eventually evolve into a platform called *VerySoul*. Inspired by Spirit, Sally and her team created a space where developing mediums could practice and cultivate authentic evidential mediumship.

I still had no intention of working professionally; I was practicing for my own spiritual development, approaching my practice with the dedication and discipline of a martial artist—knowing that when you fall, you just get back up and keep practicing.

Then one day, she said, "With the feedback you are receiving, you should do this professionally." If it weren't for Sally's encouragement, I probably wouldn't have stepped into the public arena with mediumship. I never imagined it would become my life's culminating work— offering comfort to those in grief and facilitating connections for healing. Even now, my practice continues to strengthen my own development and deepen my unfolding relationship with Spirit.

Deep gratitude fills my heart. I feel the threads of these sacred connections supporting me—Suzanne's emphasis on evidence and joy, Eileen's gentle, heart-centered way, and Sally's recognition of a potential I hadn't yet seen in myself. The luminous web that once flowed through my hands in bodywork now extends beyond physical form, connecting across the veil between worlds. My background in psychotherapy informs how I deliver difficult messages with compassion. My martial arts training gives me the discipline to stay present when connections come in fragments. And my bodywork experience attunes me to subtle energies and intuitive awareness.

Through these cherished teachers, I've come to recognize what makes a true mentor: humility, integrity, and the willingness to serve something greater than oneself. They modeled what it means to walk the path with both discipline and grace—to hold space without needing to shine, to guide without needing to lead. Now, I strive to embody those same qualities for others—offering support not as an authority, but as a fellow traveler, listening deeply to both worlds. The sensitivity once seen as a liability has become my greatest gift—not because I cultivated it alone, but because others recognized and nurtured it when I could not yet see its value. In this way, the lineage continues—not through imitation, but through presence, devotion, and the ever-deepening practice of surrender.

INVITATION TO PAUSE

- Close your eyes and feel into the lineage of love that has shaped you. Whose hands have guided yours? Whose presence opened a door in you that you didn't know existed?

- Consider the qualities you most admire in your mentors. How are you already embodying these qualities, perhaps without realizing it? Who in your life right now might benefit from having their gifts recognized and nurtured?

- Reflect on how you are already a bridge between worlds— not necessarily through mediumship, but through your unique way of sensing and serving.

- What practice or path might you explore with beginner's mind, surrendering to new possibilities?

- Allow stillness to show you: Who are you becoming through this quiet lineage of love, presence, and surrender?

HARMONIZING WITH SPIRIT

"Blending doesn't begin with will—it begins with stillness."

I hadn't planned to step away from my Rolf Structural Integration practice. But when the world shut down during the COVID pandemic, everything changed—my once-busy office fell silent. In that unexpected stillness, I began to sense a new direction unfolding. The previous year, I had attended the Arthur Findlay College of mediumship and had been taking courses with Suzanne Giesemann since 2018. Over time, the quiet that filled my days felt less like absence and more like an invitation —a chance to deepen my spiritual practice through mediumship.

As the world shifted, so did the ways we could connect and learn. My mentor, Eileen Davies, began offering her classes online, and I was fortunate to become one of her students. Since she was based in the UK, this connection would not have been possible without the unexpected circumstances of the pandemic. What initially seemed like an ending became an unforeseen bridge into a deeper devotion to mediumship.

As my mediumship practice developed, something unexpected

began to surface. The more I sat in connection with spirit, the more familiar it felt—as if my earlier experiences had quietly prepared me for this path all along, though I hadn't realized it at the time. There was a quality to the preparation, the surrender, and the way energy moved through these sessions that stirred something familiar and deep within me.

One session from that time glows bright in my memory, a moment when the connection felt especially clear. My client that day, whom I'll call Emily, longed to hear from her husband who had passed. As I prepared for our session, I found myself moving through the same ritual I'd practiced countless times before—but not in mediumship training.

I centered myself, finding a still point within. My breath deepened naturally, and I settled into a quality of attention that was both relaxed and utterly present. As I offered a silent prayer—not for my will to prevail, but for whatever wanted to come through—something clicked into place. This way of preparing, this settling into presence, was exactly how I approached stepping onto the mat in Aikido.

At first, my mind tugged at control. I found myself wanting to force a connection for Emily, to push for the proof and comfort she so desperately needed. But that familiar tightness of effort triggered another memory—my early days in the dojo, when I would stiffen against my partner's energy instead of flowing with it. Almost without thinking, I did what I'd learned to do then: I softened, released my grip on the outcome, and listened.

The shift was immediate and unmistakable. Emily's husband stepped into my awareness, his gentle presence filling the room. But what struck me wasn't just his arrival—it was the effortlessness with which the connection unfolded. My mind had gone quiet in a way I recognized but had never named in this context. In Aikido, we called it "mushin"—no-mind—that state where thinking stops and pure awareness takes over.

I began describing a garden they had tended together, the rich scent of earth on their hands, the sound of robins singing among the roses. The words flowed through me without effort, without my mental commentary getting in the way. It was the same flowing state I entered during randori, that free-form practice in martial arts training where I learned to respond to unpredictable energy without thinking, just moving with whatever came.

"Tell Em the roses still bloom, and the robin sings," I heard myself say, and I knew these weren't my words. They carried the warmth of his love, delivered through me but not from me.

Emily's sharp intake of breath brought me back to dual awareness—staying connected to her husband's presence while simultaneously witnessing her recognition. This, too, felt familiar: the way I'd learned to maintain awareness of both my partner and the entire dojo during practice, that quality of sustained attention that kept me responsive to everything at once.

"Our garden," she whispered, tears streaming. "He loved those roses, and there were always robins... How could you know that?"

As I watched Emily's face transform from grief to wonder, I felt a quiet stirring of recognition. There was something about this work—the centering, the surrender, the way I'd learned to step aside and let something greater move through me—that felt familiar, so similar to my martial arts practice.

That session with Emily stayed with me, not just for the beautiful connection she received, but for the questions it stirred. Over the following weeks, as I continued working with clients online, I began to notice this feeling of familiarity more often. Each time I prepared for a session, I moved into the same centered state I'd cultivated in the dojo for decades.

A few weeks later, another session brought this understanding into even sharper focus. A mother came to me desperate to connect with her son who had passed suddenly. As I prepared, the familiar doubts arose: What if no connection comes? What if I fail her when she needs comfort most?

Then I heard my sensei's voice from years before, as clearly as if he were sitting beside me: "When your mind is full of thoughts, there is no room to move." I breathed deeply, let go of expectation, and created space within—the same spaciousness I had learned to cultivate when facing an opponent's sudden attack.

Her son arrived with the playful energy of youth, showing me a collection of signed baseballs and filling my awareness with the sound of distinctive laughter that made his mother catch her breath in recognition. As I shared the details he offered—private jokes, a hidden note she had yet to discover—I felt the same effortless blending I knew from Aikido, a current that required no strain, only alignment and trust.

What moved me most wasn't just witnessing her son's presence, but watching this grieving mother's face as wonder gradually replaced despair. There's something about a parent's grief that touches the deepest places in us all. While I held space for her experience, inwardly I felt that familiar expansion of the heart—the same compassion that arose when I helped a struggling partner on the mat, that recognition of our shared humanity in moments of vulnerability.

As our session ended and I sat in the quiet of my office, the connections became impossible to ignore. The way I'd entered that spacious state of listening. The flow that moved through me when I stopped trying to control it. The quality of presence that allowed me to hold both her son's energy and her grief simultaneously. This wasn't just similar to my martial arts training—it was the same training, applied in a completely different realm.

The weeks that followed brought session after session where these parallels deepened. Each time I sat with a client, I found myself drawing on skills I'd cultivated on the mat, skills I'd never imagined could serve in this sacred work.

There was the afternoon I worked with an elderly man seeking his late wife, and I noticed how I instinctively bowed inwardly before beginning—the same gesture of respect I offered my training partners. The way I listened for her presence felt identical to the way I'd learned to sense an opponent's intention before they moved, that quality of open awareness that allowed me to feel shifts in energy long before they became visible.

When his wife came through with memories of their kitchen table, their morning coffee ritual, and a particular song she hummed while cooking, I recognized a quality we called "zanshin" in the dojo—that sustained awareness that keeps you connected to everything happening in the space around you. I could simultaneously feel her gentle presence, witness his recognition, and maintain my own centered state.

Another session revealed another layer of understanding. A woman came seeking her brother, and as I prepared, I felt my familiar tendency to try too hard, to push for results. But instead of forcing, I found myself doing what I'd learned to do when meeting a particularly challenging opponent: I softened completely. In Aikido, we learned that the moment you try to overpower your partner, you lose your connection to them. The same was true here—the moment I tried to force spirit communication, the connection vanished.

Slowly, a picture began forming. The "mushin" I experienced in martial arts—that state of no-mind where thinking stops and pure awareness takes over—was exactly what mediumship required. The "fudoshin," or immovable center, that kept me stable no matter what energy arose on the mat was the same quality that allowed me to remain grounded while channeling intense grief or overwhelming love.

As the months passed and my understanding deepened, I began to sense that many of the principles I'd learned in the dojo were quietly preparing me for this most sacred work. The beginner's mind that kept me open to learning new techniques was the same openness that allowed me to receive messages I could never have imagined. The way I'd learned to blend with a partner's energy rather than resist it was identical to how I needed to harmonize with the spirits who came through.

Perhaps most important was realizing that both paths seemed to be about the same thing: getting my ego, my agenda, my need to control out of the way so something greater could flow through. Whether I was blending with an opponent's attack or opening to a spirit's message, the moment I tried to force an outcome with my own will, I lost the connection entirely.

One evening, as I finished a particularly moving session where a grandfather had come through with such specific details about his woodworking shop that his daughter wept with recognition, I sat in the quiet stillness of my office and understood. The pandemic hadn't ended one path and begun another—it had revealed that I'd been walking the same path all along. My body and mind, once trained to redirect physical force with harmony and love, were now channeling the power of love in realms unseen. The dojo and my quiet room were both sacred spaces where I practiced the same fundamental art: the art of becoming transparent to something larger than myself.

Invitation to Pause

- Consider a situation where you are holding tight to an outcome, a relationship, a way things "should" be or "should have been." What new possibilities might open if you moved into flowing with what is instead?
- Reflect on the moments when you've been a bridge for others—when your presence, not your words, created connection. How might you trust that same capacity to connect across any distance, any difference?
- What if your greatest strength isn't in what you can make happen, but in how completely you can get out of the way? What wants to flow through you when you become transparent to love?

THE SILENT FLAME

The heart that empties itself becomes
a mirror for the infinite.

Unless there's an instant awakening, entering a flow state is not shaped in a single moment but carved slowly over time—and it continues to deepen. Whether through music, art, martial arts, or mediumship, the path begins with learning forms and techniques. Yet, at some point, the practice calls for the release of everything we've learned. I continue to discover that surrender is the key to entering a state of no mind, merging with the deeper currents of the universe.

In my martial arts training—now spanning over forty-four years—I've witnessed this again and again. In mediumship, I find the same truth: the moment I stop trying, letting go of effort and expectation, everything changes. In Aikido, there comes a time when the form disappears, and only flow remains—no mind, no tension, just movement arising from presence. The same threshold reveals itself in mediumship. Connection doesn't come through trying or technique but through surrender to what arises in the moment. The more I soften, the more clearly the messages flow through. I've noticed this with clients as well—the more they soften, the more fully they're able to receive.

Each session offers a new opportunity to practice surrender and presence. Today, I sat with a mother whose son had slipped from this world two seasons past, leaving her heart an open wound. I felt her longing before she arrived—a quiet ache that settled in my chest like a stone polished by the rush of a river. As I prepared, drawing on everything I've learned about stillness and flow, my breath softened. A flicker of effort arose in my awareness—that old urge to push for results—and I let it dissolve with an exhale. Be still. Notice what arises. A prayer formed: "Let me be transparent—so transparent that love may shine through."

As I let go, I sensed a young man in my awareness, his presence like sunlight breaking through clouds, his energy warm and gentle. I felt his laughter, his joy: a team in red uniforms, a baseball glove in his hands. A sense of passing quickly underwater—cold, then release, then peace—his grandfather's steady presence nearby, watching over him.

"He's showing me a baseball team—red uniforms," I shared with his mother, my voice soft. "I feel cold, an accident...water." Her breath caught. I continued, guided by what came: "He's showing yellow flowers—they're connected to the anniversary of his passing. He wants you to know he's okay. He wants to be remembered with joy rather than sadness, if possible; he wants to share his joy." I saw a group of his best friends at his memorial. The air between us seemed to hold something beyond grief—a quiet resonance of recognition and reunion.

As our session unfolded, I witnessed a subtle transformation in her. The rigid posture of grief that had characterized her body when she first sat down gradually softened, like ice yielding to spring's gentle warmth. By the time we concluded, tears still traced paths down her cheeks, but they seemed different now—a gentle release of a heart beginning to breathe again. Her eyes, which had been downcast and clouded with sorrow, now held a flicker of something new, perhaps the first tender shoot of acceptance taking root.

As our session ended, I understood something deeper about this work: it was about becoming a clear vessel, far more than technique or any special skill. All of it had led to this: learning to disappear so completely that only love remained. I know this is not a destination but a direction I continue to move toward.

Just as trees on the bank of a lake are reflected in the water, so too are all things—the living, the departed, joy, and sorrow—reflected in the vast mirror of consciousness. My teacher used to say, "Be inwardly still, and the whole world becomes still. Be inwardly agitated, and the whole world burns." Those words found their deepest truth in these connections with loved ones unseen, where a centered presence becomes the still point from which all perception flows.

I recall another session when no voice came for long minutes, my mind twitching to press forward. Instead, I settled into the quiet, and a grandmother's voice broke through, soft and sure, with a message that left her daughter weeping with relief. I have been learning to trust the rhythm—sometimes a rush of visions, sometimes a single whisper—knowing each arrives as it must.

In the quiet that followed, deeper questions began to surface: "What is this 'I' that moves, that listens, that speaks?" The question had arisen after countless sessions, a faint echo from years of pondering. Once, I thought myself the warrior, the doer, the one who shaped the world with hands and will. But the years slowly burned away this illusion, revealing a deeper truth: there is no separate "I" to claim these acts. The baseball field, the red uniforms, the joy—they were not mine to conjure, nor a son mine to summon. They arose from the same vast stillness that holds everything—a stillness that is not empty but full, not silent but alive with all that is.

The silence of those locked-down days deepened this understanding, closing one gate but opening another. I would sit then, as I do now, feeling the same life force that once flowed through my hands now stretching beyond touch, a radiant current linking my awareness to the unseen. Each connection echoed an insight glimpsed long ago: the greatest ease comes when we move with the current, not against it. For me, that means being clear as water, a vessel so transparent that something greater can shine through.

What I hope shines through is Love itself, that presence of pure awareness. In this sacred witnessing, a mother who mourns, the son she loves, and the field he plays in—they are reflections in the mirror of consciousness, fleeting yet eternal, born of the same divine light we all are. Ultimately, there is no separation, no loss, only the play of Love appearing as many, then returning to One.

When the session is finished, and a mother's heart is touched by a peace I had the privilege to witness, I let the room hold me in its emptiness. I breathe in the scent of the extinguished candle—that brief moment when smoke holds both the memory of flame and the promise of its return. What seems most solid is often most transient, and what seems most ethereal—love, consciousness, connection—endures beyond all forms.

Like the final movement in a martial form returning to center, I return to stillness—the source and destination of all paths.

In both disciplines, I have come to a similar understanding: our greatest strength lies in harmonious flow, not in grasping but in allowing, not in separation but in the recognition that all boundaries are ultimately illusory.

Perhaps you've glimpsed this too—a moment when letting go revealed more than striving ever could, when abiding in stillness opened a door to the vast. This weave of yielding strength, centered presence, and boundless awareness is no mere craft—it is a way of being, a path of resting in Love's silent flame.

INVITATION TO PAUSE

- Have you ever experienced a moment when silence revealed more than words could offer?
- What does surrender mean in your life—not as giving up, but as giving in to something greater than yourself?

- How do you listen—beyond thought, beyond effort—for the quiet voice of love?
- Is there a place in your heart, or in your past, where grief still lingers? What might it feel like to rest with it, not to fix or force, but simply to witness with tenderness?
- In what areas of your life might you be trying too hard, where stepping back and allowing natural flow could reveal new possibilities?

GOLD NUGGETS

"Nothing real is ever taken.
Love, once awakened, cannot be undone."

As my mediumship practice has deepened, I realize that the common ground I once recognized between martial arts and mediumship was just the beginning. Each day that I have the honor of sitting with a client and sharing these sacred communications fills me with gratitude, joy, wonder, and awe.

Loved ones in spirit offer golden nuggets—evidence so precise it leaves no doubt that their love endures. These golden moments arrive in their own time—sometimes only validated weeks after the session has ended—surprising me as much as those who receive them.

I continue to discover that the more I step aside, let go, and surrender into wonder, the more clearly these miracles shine through.

The privilege of accompanying loved ones through grief and witnessing the healing that unfolds through these connections is deeply humbling. Now, as I reach my "golden years," it feels like the perfect culmination of my life in service to Spirit.

Sometimes, love doesn't arrive with thunder but with the quiet precision of a single, undeniable detail.

WHEN LOVE SPEAKS IN DETAILS

One day, a young woman sat with me for a session, her presence both excited and tentative. "Do you have anyone in spirit you hope to hear from?" I asked. "Not really—I am just curious," she replied, "I don't have anybody." I was surprised by this answer—how could this session unfold if she knew no one who had passed? Then she added, "Well, I have a grandma and grandpa, but I didn't know them well."

I wondered how this would possibly unfold, but I let go and said, "Let's see what happens," releasing my need to know. To our surprise, her grandfather in spirit arrived, clear and bright, announcing his name. Then he gave me an image of a stop sign. "There's a story about a stop sign," I said. Her eyes widened. "That's what I think of when I think of him," she exclaimed. Later, she shared how he would put the car in park every time he came to a stop sign, a habit from years of driving a car with a manual transmission.

We both laughed at this perfect memory—her grandfather had found the one thread she would recognize, a golden nugget that bridged their connection despite limited shared experiences. I felt that familiar wave of amazement, watching her face light up with recognition. Even across the thinnest threads of shared experience, love finds a way.

Another session brought a mother grieving her son, who had passed in an accident. As I centered myself, drawing on the stillness I had learned to cultivate, I saw an ambulance, felt his presence, and knew he had not passed instantly. "But he didn't regain consciousness," I said, sensing the weight of this information. "This matters because she had to make the most painful decision to allow the machines to be turned off." Tears welled in her eyes as I shared that he wanted her to know she had made the right choice. He was grateful for her love and strength to let him go.

Then he showed me stars—tiny points of light—like Tinker Bell's glow. "Tinker Bell?" I said. "I feel like I just saw Tinker Bell go through my awareness." "That was his dog's name," she said, "gone with him in the crash." Both of us sat in awe of how her son had created such a clear message. These unexpected, specific details carry the most healing power precisely because they couldn't be guessed or researched. There is no other explanation.

WHEN SPIRIT'S TIMING UNFOLDS—NO TURNS INTO YES!

What continues to humble me is how these golden moments often unfold beyond the session itself. Spirit operates on a different timeline than our expectations, planting seeds that blossom when they're most needed.

During that same session with the grieving mother, her son made me aware of something she could not verify until weeks later. "He is showing me a red-and-white flag," I said. "Do you understand this?" She replied no. "Now he has me looking up into a blue sky, and I see a red-and-white flag in the sky. Would you understand this?" Again, she answered no. I gently encouraged her, "Just write it down—we'll see if it makes sense later."

Two weeks later, on his birthday, she sent me an email with a photo. She had been walking, missing him deeply, when she looked up and saw an airplane trailing a red-and-white banner across the sky. It read: "Wawa"—the name of the store they used to walk to together. He had always laughed about it. "Such a silly name," he'd say, "it makes me laugh." That banner was a whisper of love, arriving exactly when it could be felt most deeply.

IN ANOTHER SESSION with a different mother whose son had passed, I received two distinct images. "I'm seeing a phoenix," I told her, "and also a heart." Later, she shared about a phoenix tattoo she had gotten after her son's passing—with a heart underneath it. In the same session, I heard a name. "He's saying Brian, but he's telling me it's not spelled B-R-I-A-N, it's spelled B-R-Y-A-N." She looked puzzled and said she didn't know anyone by that name.

Just minutes after our session concluded, she sent me an email: "It just hit me—my daughter is getting married in three months, and her new surname will be BRYAN!" These moments remind me that those in spirit see a larger tapestry than we do, weaving evidence through time and revealing its meaning when we're ready to receive it.

MESSAGES THAT BRIDGE HEARTS

Sometimes, the gold nuggets aren't meant for the person sitting with me, but someone else. A mother, receiving messages rich with connection, was puzzled by two details. "He says his grandfather was a doctor of optometry," I offered.

"No," she replied.

"And Lewis Street?"

Again, "No."

My thinking mind leapt in—had I misheard? Was this my imagination? But I had learned to trust the process, even when I couldn't understand it.

Later, she wrote to me: her husband had confirmed his father had indeed trained as a doctor of optometry but never worked as an optometrist—he worked for Boeing in optics! And Lewis Street was the street where his favorite aunt had lived. Those nuggets weren't for her but for him—a gift from their son, bridging father and mother in love's embrace.

These moments remind me that spirit communication serves purposes beyond what I can see. Those in spirit remain aware of our interconnected lives and relationships, often perceiving a bigger picture than we ourselves can grasp.

THE HUMOR OF LOVE

It is such a joyful experience when those in spirit sometimes show up with their humor. Two sisters in their late seventies scheduled their first-ever mediumship session with me. Right away, their father in spirit joined us, telling me he was from Palermo and his wife from Milan. He showed me he had been a shopkeeper, and I kept seeing images of sewing.

"I'm seeing something like upholstery work," I said. "It looks like sewing on an arm, like a couch." The sisters giggled and said, "No, not upholstery." I laughed too, realizing how my mind's attempt to interpret clouds the message. But spirit continues to guide the essence through.

As we were saying our goodbyes after what had been a joyful reunion with their parents, their father stepped forward one last time, and I heard a single word: "Shoemaker." The sisters burst into laughter —their father had indeed been a shoemaker in Palermo, and the sewing I had seen was for leather, not furniture! These moments of clarity often arrive only when I stop trying to interpret and fully allow the communication to flow.

Those in spirit continue to surprise me with their playful persistence. In another reading, a man arrived, showing me a tattoo on his forearm. "Pink Panther," I said, seeing the playful image. His brother smiled softly. "It's a panther," he clarified, "not pink, but he had it right there on his forearm." Even with a slight misinterpretation, strong evidence came through—those in spirit often highlight what will be most recognizable, even if the details arrive through impression rather than precision. The essence was there—a panther tattoo—and it was unmistakable.

Another time, a stepdad came through, and I heard the name Sue. "Do you recognize the name Sue?" I asked. She replied, "No." Then I heard the stepdad in spirit say: "Not a girl named Sue—a boy named Sue! Johnny Cash!" And then I heard Johnny Cash music playing. His stepdaughter laughed, "We used to tease him about his playing Johnny Cash music all the time—he played those songs constantly." These tender threads, stitched with humor and heart, remind me how those in spirit perceive what I cannot, offering nuggets that spark recognition and wonder.

When Healing Meets Resistance

The transformative power of these golden moments becomes most apparent when they reach someone in the depths of grief. Such was the case with Thomas, who arrived skeptical but desperate. Two years after losing his daughter to leukemia, the grief continued to overwhelm him. As he sat rigidly across from me, arms crossed defensively, I recognized the posture of someone steeled against pain.

Drawing on everything I had learned about not meeting force with force, I softened into his resistance rather than confronting it. "I understand your doubts," I told him. "They're natural and even healthy. You don't need to believe anything I say. Just observe and draw your own conclusions."

His shoulders lowered slightly—the first yielding.

As I centered myself, I felt a gentle presence—a ray of sunshine breaking through clouds, the scent of strawberries. "There is a young lady here showing me a book with pressed flowers inside... violets, I think. And she's laughing about ice cream that melted all over a car seat —chocolate, with some kind of candy mixed in."

Thomas's breath caught. "Her journal," he whispered. "She pressed violets in her journal. And on her last good day, I bought her favorite— chocolate ice cream with peanut butter cups. It melted before we got home." As he spoke, his rigid posture began to soften, his crossed arms gradually relaxing—a physical manifestation of grief beginning to yield to connection.

The Continuing Wonder

Each session teaches me anew that these golden nuggets arrive unbidden, often beyond my grasp until their meaning unfolds. Whether it's a stop sign tale, a tattooed panther, or a melody from decades past, they flow through when I step aside completely—when I remember that my role is simply to yield to those in spirit, allowing Love to speak its luminous language.

The learning continues, and that is part of the wonder and joy. I am honored to steward these communications, discovering daily that Love's vast embrace requires only a humble heart willing to let go. Perhaps you, too, have felt a similar nudge—to trust what whispers now, knowing its truth may shine later, a golden thread of Love woven through the silence.

INVITATION TO PAUSE

- Have you ever received a message, sign, or memory that felt like more than coincidence—something quietly meant just for you?
- Recall a moment when an unexpected detail brought comfort or clarity. What made it feel true?
- Have you ever dismissed something small, only to understand its deeper meaning later? What shifted in you when that understanding came?
- Consider how love might speak—not always in loud declarations, but in small, shimmering hints. Are you open to noticing the golden threads woven through your own life?
- Where might Spirit be trying to reach you now—not through certainty, but through trust?

LINES OF CONNECTION

"I don't draw what I see—I surrender to what asks to be seen."

I never considered myself a sketch artist. My hands had learned to sense the subtle patterns of fascia, to blend with an Aikido partner's energy, to hold space for grief—but not to draw portraits. Yet in retrospect, I see how these practices were preparing me in unexpected ways. Each required releasing conscious control, yielding to something beyond the analytical mind. In the early days of my mediumship practice, I began making simple sketches during sessions, as a way to occupy my analytical mind so my heart could speak more clearly. These initial drawings were rudimentary at best—stick figures and basic shapes that reflected my complete lack of formal training. At the time, I saw them merely as tools for entering a flow state, not as evidence I might offer.

That changed dramatically during a reading for a mother whose son had crossed to spirit. As I connected with her son Jon, I found myself absently sketching as usual, making marks that held no particular meaning to me. Suddenly, I felt a distinct shift in the energy—a gentle but unmistakable presence directing my attention.

"Stop," I heard clearly in my awareness. "Turn the paper over and start again, and let go."

I paused, surprised by the directness of this communication.

"This time, relax and let the energy flow," he continued. "Just let it come through you. Don't try, just let it flow."

Something in the instruction resonated deeply with the surrender I had practiced in other areas of my life. I turned the paper over as directed, took a deep breath, and allowed my hand to move across the page with no conscious intention. Jon's mother said, "Wow!" as she too noticed the energy shift when I began sketching freely. The charcoal pencil seemed to move of its own accord, whispering across the page, creating lines and shadows that emerged without planning or effort on my part.

When I finished and looked down at what had appeared on the page, I was surprised to see a beautiful face looking back at me—one I did not recognize, yet rendered with a detail and nuance I had never achieved before. I showed the sketch to Jon's mom at the end of our session.

"That's Jon," she whispered. "He was an artist who loved drawing portraits."

In that moment, I understood that Jon had not just been the subject of the drawing—he had been its co-creator, using my hand as his instrument. By letting go, by not trying, I surrendered into the flow, allowing the sketch to emerge. I became a vessel for something greater than myself.

SINCE THAT PIVOTAL SESSION, this unexpected form of mediumship has become a regular part of my practice. I approach each drawing with the same invitation Jon first gave me: "Relax and let go." I have no awareness of what image will emerge as I draw during a reading. My hand moves across the page while I continue to share the messages and evidence coming through from Spirit. There is no conscious effort, no visualization of their loved one—only surrender to the process.

What continues to astonish me and my clients is how often these drawings bear a striking resemblance to photographs I have never seen. The emotional impact of these moments is profound. Recently, a mother who had received a sketch during her session showed it to her son afterward. Upon seeing the drawing, he burst into tears, exclaiming, "That's my grandma!" These raw, unfiltered reactions happen frequently —clients gasp or shed tears when they recognize the familiar tilt of a head, the characteristic smile, or the essence of their loved one captured in a few simple lines. Some have told me they frame these sketches, keeping them as special treasures—tangible reminders of the enduring connection with those they love.

I've noticed that these drawings offer something my verbal messages alone cannot—a physical, visual touchstone clients can return to again and again. While spoken messages comfort in the moment, the sketches provide lasting evidence—something that can be held. In a process that can otherwise feel ephemeral, this tangible reminder becomes a bridge between worlds. Clients have shared how receiving a sketch has helped transform their grief—offering a visible thread of connection they can revisit. The drawing becomes not just a memento, but a doorway—a visible whisper of love.

Sometimes the connections are even more surprising. During one reading, I completed a drawing that the client did not immediately recognize. Later, she sent me a message with a photograph attached— the sketch perfectly captured her only living relative, along with a message: "We are forever connected in Love."

Beyond the immediate recognition, there's something even more intriguing about these spirit-guided portraits. What I've noticed about these sketches is that each one has a unique feeling. It may be conveyed through the eyes, the mouth, or a tilt of the head, but it is more than that—each portrait seems to carry its own distinctive energy. No sketch looks like the others, and there is no consistent style; what appears seems to shift with each spirit connection.

Another curious pattern has emerged in these spirit-inspired portraits. When clients later share photographs of their loved ones, we often discover that some of the drawings appear as mirror images—the tilt of the head opposite, or the face turned in the reverse direction of the photograph. It's as if those in spirit are showing me their reflection, perhaps like a mirror image, suggesting how the veil between worlds acts as a kind of sacred mirror. This mirroring effect reminds me that spirit communication traverses dimensions we can barely comprehend, where our usual understanding of space and perspective may not apply. These mirrored images offer yet another piece of evidence that what emerges on the page isn't coming from my own memory or imagination.

WHEN I WAS YOUNGER, around eighteen, I had taken some painting classes, but I never studied drawing or learned portraiture techniques. Before Jon's intervention, my ability with a pencil extended no further than simple doodles—certainly not realistic human faces. Yet now, through surrender to the process, images emerge that I could never create through skill or effort alone. When clients express amazement at the likenesses, I always clarify that I cannot take credit for what appears on the page. These drawings come through me, not from me—a humbling reminder that I am simply a conduit for the love and evidence spirit wishes to share.

This unexpected artistic dimension of my practice has revealed something profound about the nature of spirit communication. The sketches don't arise from visualization or conscious effort. My hand moves, often without awareness of what's taking shape, while I remain attuned to spirit's presence. I'm frequently surprised by the features that emerge—faces I've never seen, rendered through lines I didn't intend. It's as if Spirit bypasses my mind and guides my hand directly. In these moments, mediumship becomes more than communication—it becomes a direct expression, a dissolving of boundaries between human and spirit. Each drawing is not the product of technique, but of receptivity—bearing the unmistakable signature of something beyond me.

JON CONTINUES to be a presence in this work, and I silently thank him each time I pick up a pencil before a session. His patient instruction —"Don't try, just let it flow"—has become a mantra not just for drawing but for all aspects of my mediumship practice. What began with his gentle guidance has evolved into a profound dimension of my work, one that continues to surprise me with each session. While my verbal communications with spirit require translation and interpretation, these drawings seem to bypass those filters entirely, allowing for a more direct expression of presence and recognition.

In the simple act of releasing control, of trusting the unseen guidance at work through my hand, I've discovered yet another dimension of how Love transcends the boundary between worlds—manifesting in unexpected ways when I step aside and simply allow it to flow. Jon's lesson has deepened over time, teaching me that mediumship is not about trying harder, but about surrendering more completely—creating a clear channel through which Spirit's love and messages can unfold unimpeded. Each drawing becomes a visible testament to the truth I continue to discover: that Love endures, presence transcends form, and Love finds its way—etched in lines that never fade.

Surrendering Into Love

Tammy Lee Anderson

Families often ask to see examples of these spirit-guided sketches compared to photographs of their loved ones. A gallery showcasing these sketches—where permission has been given—can be viewed at the Gallery of Sketches at:

⊕ **healingwellness.com**

INVITATION TO PAUSE

- Where in your life might you need to "turn the paper over and begin again"? What creative expression or gift might be waiting to flow through you if you let go?
- Recall a time when your best work came not through effort, but through flow. What conditions allowed that natural expression to emerge?
- Consider where in your life you might now release control and let go of the outcome. What might Spirit be trying to show you—not through your will, but through your willingness?
- When you attune to life with humility, what becomes clearer?

THE MOUNTAIN'S SURRENDER

"The real ascent is inward—
each step a letting go, each breath a prayer"

The trail stretched before us like a question mark, winding through ancient sequoias toward a summit we could not yet see. Mount Whitney —14,505 feet of granite challenge rising from the Sierra Nevada range— waited in silence as our small group of four began the journey from Mineral King in the southern part of Sequoia National Park. Our eight-day trek would traverse some of California's most breathtaking wilderness, from the west side of the Sierra Nevada to Whitney Portal on the east. I had trained for months, filled my pack with carefully chosen gear, and strengthened my body for the challenge ahead. But I hadn't antici-pated how quickly the mountain would strip away my preparation and bring me to my knees.

I had embarked on many journeys in my life—into the depths of bodywork, through the circular movements of Aikido, across waters in my kayak—but this mountain trek called to me as something more than a physical challenge. As I prepared my gear and trained my body, I sensed that Whitney would become both an outer and inner pilgrimage. Like many before me who sought wisdom on mountaintops, I was drawn not just to test my endurance but to listen for the quiet teachings that emerge when we leave behind comfort and routine. What I couldn't have known then was how completely the mountain would strip away my illusions of control and reveal that true strength often begins with surrender.

"The mountains are calling, and I must go," John Muir once wrote. What he didn't say was that mountains sometimes call us not to conquest, but to surrender.

That first day was ambitious—perhaps too ambitious. We pushed on from Mineral King through Sawtooth Pass, as the trail climbed steeply through sand and rocks and seemingly endless switchbacks, hiking past 11,800 feet, gaining altitude so rapidly that my body had no time to adjust to the thinning air. By late afternoon, as shadows stretched long across the trail, something inside me began to shift. A dull throb behind my eyes grew steadily into a hammer's rhythm, each heartbeat a painful pulse. My steps, confident hours before, became uncertain.

"I'm fine," I insisted to my friends, though the words sounded hollow even to my own ears. "Just need to catch my breath."

But breath was precisely what was becoming elusive at this altitude. As we continued toward our first camp after passing through Sawtooth Pass, my vision narrowed to the few feet of trail before me. One foot, then another. The pack that had felt manageable that morning now seemed to carry stones instead of supplies. The setting sun painted the surrounding peaks in gold and crimson glory, but I could barely lift my eyes to see it.

Darkness had fallen by the time we reached camp on the east side of the mountain, and by then, I could no longer pretend. The altitude sickness had fully claimed me—the worst headache of my life pounding behind my eyes, my body trembling with chills despite the summer air, nausea rising with each shallow breath. As my friends quickly set up camp, I sank to the ground, wondering if this journey had ended before it truly began.

"I don't know if I can make it," I whispered as they wrapped me in sleeping bags, my body shaking uncontrollably. One friend rummaged through his pack for altitude medication. I couldn't even stomach tea, forcing myself to eat a small piece of an energy bar just so I could take the medicine without throwing up. My friends worked quickly, one heating water, all three surrounding me with care I was too sick to properly acknowledge.

Through the misery, a thought surfaced—how quickly the mountain had humbled me. All my preparation, all my determined self-sufficiency, meant nothing to these ancient peaks. Here, at the edge of the Kern River Valley beneath a canopy of stars I was too ill to appreciate, I faced a truth I had encountered in other forms throughout my life: some things cannot be conquered through will alone.

That night, as pain and cold fought for dominance in my trembling body, I remembered other surrenders—the infant struggling for first breath, the Aikido student learning to yield rather than resist, the structural integration therapist understanding that true healing comes from listening to the body's wisdom rather than imposing will upon it. Again and again, life had taught me that true strength often begins with acceptance rather than resistance.

So there, on the hard ground of our hastily-made camp, I surrendered—not to defeat, but to the mountain's wisdom. I accepted that my body needed what it needed, that no amount of determination could override the physical realities of altitude and oxygen. I let go of expectations, of pushing through, of proving something. I simply allowed myself to be ill, to be cared for—to be human.

Morning came with tentative mercy. I opened my eyes to alpenglow painting distant peaks, the headache had receded to a dull memory. My friends watched anxiously as I slowly sat up, took a careful breath, then another. The nausea had passed. My body, given time to adjust and the care it needed, had found its equilibrium with the altitude.

"Better?" one friend asked, offering a steaming cup of coffee.

"Yes," I said, and meant it. "I think I can continue."

And so we did—seven more days of breathtaking beauty and challenge across the Sierra Nevada range. The High Sierra Trail from Sawtooth Pass to Kern River Valley descends to 7,800 feet. Then, hiking north, the elevation stays around 7,800 to 8,000 feet before ascending to Guitar Lake. Descending to the Kern River Valley (7,800 feet), we crossed crystal streams and alpine meadows, navigated narrow passages and sweeping vistas. We watched sunsets turn mountains to fire and dawns break over landscapes few ever witness.

The mountain offered another powerful lesson. We stopped to rest under a piñon pine, its gnarled branches a testament to years of endurance in this harsh landscape. The stillness was profound—a cool wind, and in that quiet, I felt the mountain's presence as a teacher whose lessons required me to listen rather than speak. While hiking, our trail guide encountered a rattlesnake on the trail—and to my dismay, quickly killed it. I watched, disturbed by the unnecessary taking of life in the animal's own home, remembering Bear's teachings about respecting all beings as relations.

✦

This reaction was born from a profound experience years earlier while living in a desert monastery. There, rattlesnakes were common companions on the trails, initially filling me with fear. One day, I came face to face with a rattlesnake, and in that moment of mutual recognition, we had what I can only describe as a conversation of consciousness.

I acknowledged my fear to the snake, and somehow understood its response: "I am also afraid. That is why I recommend you carry a walking stick when hiking so I can easily feel your vibration. When you come near, I will rattle to signal I am near, and then we will agree to bow to each other and go our way." From that day forward, I carried a walking stick on hikes, announcing my presence to all creatures. Each time I encountered a rattlesnake, there was a mutual respect—a silent agreement to share the space peacefully before parting ways. The snake had become my teacher in respect and honor.

So when our trail guide killed the rattlesnake on the trail toward the summit, my heart hurt to see this animal killed in its own territory for no reason. Something in me couldn't let that death pass without acknowledgment.

Honoring the indigenous wisdom that had always resonated with me—that life taken requires respect and purpose, that relationship extends to every creature—I surprised both myself and my friends when, unwilling to let the creature's death be meaningless, I decided to take it into my own body. As I cooked the snake over our small campfire, its scent mingling with the pine and earth, I thought of honoring life's sacredness. This act was a silent prayer to the snake, my friend and teacher, a promise that its life would nourish mine, a recognition that we are all part of the same web, where even loss can weave connection.

On the evening of the seventh night, navigating by our headlamps, we experienced hail and wet snow pummeling us as we reached Guitar Lake, elevation 11,500 feet, where we would spend our last night of this big adventure. The landscape had changed dramatically as we climbed above the tree line and our surroundings became completely rocky terrain, almost like I would imagine the moon to look. Snow flurries and cold greeted us as we arrived at our last camp, and we began to quickly set up our tents.

The next morning, we were treated to a clear day as we prepared to climb to the summit of Mount Whitney.

This would be our eighth and final day, on the High Sierra Trail. We made our ascent from Guitar Lake, near the base of Mount Whitney on the west side, and began to ascend the Trail Crest. From here we only had 2.4 miles to go to reach the summit of Mount Whitney. The trail was mostly covered in slippery ice for the first hour due to the many small springs and the previous night's snow. As we started up the steep switchbacks, only a mile into the hike, we were already above 12,000 feet of elevation, and the thin air was very challenging. Only 1.5 miles later we had quickly surpassed the 13,000 feet mark. The altitude made it hard to breathe, forcing us to stop and catch our breath at nearly every switchback.

Eventually, though, we stood together on Whitney's summit, with nothing but sky above and all of California spread out below, at 14,505 feet, the highest point in the contiguous United States. We had clear views of both the desert-like Owens Valley on one side and the entire alpine Sierra on the other. We could even see the western border of the Sierra, the Great Western Divide. Standing there, I felt small yet connected to something vast—not unlike that sensation years earlier in my kayak when the water held me in perfect balance between effort and grace.

The Sierra stars had been our constant companions each night of our journey—so brilliant and numerous underneath the clear mountain sky that they made you want to stay quiet in reverence. Their beauty spoke of mysteries beyond our understanding, a silent reminder of our place in this vast universe. Each evening, as we rested our tired bodies, those stars offered perspective that no words could capture.

After resting at the top, we began our long descent down the east side of the mountain. Navigating the infamous 99 switchbacks that zigzag down the mountain face on the east side, we passed a particularly precarious part of the trail marked with cables at the edge of a drop-off straight down. We continued the descent of 6,000 feet, each turn bringing us closer to the Owens Valley far below. Darkness fell as we continued our trek, knees and body aching, and soon we were navigating by headlamps, their narrow beams of light illuminating only fragments of the wet trail. Each step became a meditation in itself—the weight shifting, the foot searching for solid ground, the body responding to what was rather than what I wished it to be.

As we descended, my friend walked just ahead of me, her pack a shadowy silhouette against the deeper darkness beyond. In one heart-stopping moment, her foot slipped on the slick rock. She began to fall toward what we both knew was a sheer cliff drop.

Without thought, my hand shot out and grabbed her pack, arresting her momentum just as she teetered on the edge. In that split second between balance and catastrophe, I felt something beyond my own strength flow through me—the same current that had carried me through altitude sickness days earlier, the same flow I had felt in Aikido when turning with an opponent's energy rather than against it. We stood frozen for a moment, breathing hard, before continuing in silence, now hyperaware of each step and each other's presence. Her eyes met mine, wide with shock and gratitude, and she whispered, "Thank you." In that shared breath, our eyes met in mutual recognition of something larger than ourselves—a reminder that we walk this earth not as isolated travelers but as threads in an intricate tapestry of support and care.

This is what we do for each other as we walk this sometimes challenging trail of life. My friends had wrapped me in sleeping bags when I shivered with altitude sickness; now I reached out a hand when it was needed. The mountain had taught us both lessons in vulnerability and connection—that sometimes we give support, and sometimes we receive it, but we're never truly separate in our journey.

The summit, magnificent as it was, holds less prominence in my memory than that first night of surrender and the events of our final day. The mountain had offered its first lesson before I had barely begun the journey—that sometimes our greatest strength lies not in pushing forward but in yielding to what is.

Later that night at camp, the stars impossibly bright above us, I reflected on the experience of that day—the exhaustion, the close call, the realization that extended beyond just the two of us—that we are all connected, all responsible for catching each other when paths grow treacherous. It was the luminous web—the interconnection where every thread affects every other, where we are not separate beings but nodes in a vast network of relationship.

✦

This is the wisdom of mountains and rivers, of breath and spirit—that surrender is not abandonment of the journey but sometimes the only way to continue it. Eight days on Whitney's trails deepened what a lifetime of experiences had been teaching me: that when we release our grip on how things "should" be and accept how they are, we open ourselves to unexpected grace. That we need each other. That all life deserves respect.

Our 72-mile journey had taken us across terrain as varied as life itself —sometimes steep and demanding every ounce of effort, sometimes gentle as we crossed flower-filled meadows where the Sierra light danced across grasses. There were treacherous passages where loose scree threatened to slide beneath our boots, and moments so intense we could focus only on one step at a time, each footfall a meditation. We found respite by crystalline mountain streams, the taste of that sweet water unlike anything from a tap or bottle—alive with minerals and the mountain's essence. In those moments of rest, simply breathing in and breathing out, the mountain spoke its deepest lessons—that the path itself, with all its challenges and beauty, is the teacher.

Like our lives, the changing trail conditions offered us challenge, beauty, and everything in between. The mountain didn't discriminate— it simply presented what was, leaving us to choose how we would respond. Some sections called for determination and grit, others for appreciation and wonder, still others for caution and discernment. And there were times, especially during our night descent down those 99 switchbacks, when the best we could do was simply take one more step, then another, and another—a lesson in perseverance when the path seems longest and the destination furthest from view.

Like life itself, sometimes all we can do is take one more step, one step at a time. In those moments, when the summit seems impossible or the descent unending, the wisdom lies not in grand strategy but in the humble commitment to the next single step. This too, the mountain taught me—that sometimes surrender means releasing our attachment to swift progress or clear vision, and instead honoring the simple courage it takes to keep moving forward, however slowly, into the darkness that holds both our fears and our becoming.

Looking back now, I see that Mount Whitney was never just a physical peak to be climbed, but a living metaphor for my spiritual journey. The altitude sickness that humbled me on that first night reflected the many times life brought me to my knees, only to teach me that true strength emerges in vulnerability. The varied terrain—from meadows to ridges, from streams to scree—mirrored the diverse landscapes of my soul that I would traverse through decades of seeking. The summit offered not conquest but perspective, a brief moment to see beyond horizons usually hidden. And the descent in darkness showed me that even when we cannot see the path clearly, we can still move forward with faith, one careful step at a time.

✦

The mountain stands in my memory, not as a conquest achieved but as a teacher embraced, much like the Andes would later become for me. In its towering presence, I found again the paradoxical truth that has shaped my life—that our most profound strength often emerges precisely when we surrender our illusion of control and open ourselves to something greater than our limited understanding. There on those granite slopes, as in so many moments before and since—from the kayak's balance to the dojo's circular movements to my years as a structural integration therapist—I discovered that sometimes the path forward begins with letting go, while reaching out to catch those beside us.

Now, as I write this story and remember its lessons, I have entered life's descent in my physical form. My body no longer embodies the strong athletic form it once was—the kayaker who could slice through water at dawn, the martial artist who could blend with any energy, the hiker who could summit peaks despite altitude's challenge. Yet there is beauty in this descent too, a wisdom that comes only from the higher vantage point of a life fully lived. And what a view this life has offered me! From this elevation, I can see the patterns, the connections between seemingly separate experiences—how each challenge and surrender prepared me for the next.

The path has come full circle. My life's work and experiences have culminated in my current service as a spiritual medium—a final offering that integrates all that came before into a channel of love and healing. The structural integration therapist's understanding of the body's interconnected web, the Aikido practitioner's awareness of energy, the meditator's capacity for presence—all now flow through me as I bridge worlds and offer healing in a new form. Just last week, I sat with a mother grieving, as her son conveyed messages of love and ongoing connection from across the veil—including mention of a phoenix tattoo she had placed on her leg in his honor, and even sharing a laugh I could clearly hear. I felt the same flow that saved my friend on that cliff, the same current that carried me through Whitney's first night. From that first night of altitude sickness on Sawtooth Pass to the final steps of our 72-mile trek, the lesson remains the same—surrender is not about giving up, but about opening to something greater, something that connects us all in ways we can barely comprehend but can certainly feel when we allow ourselves to be truly present.

As I continue my descent now—not from a mountain peak but through life's later chapters—I find myself returning to the quiet of early mornings, to the stillness that has always been my truest home. In that silence, I hear again the echoes of all those who have walked beside me, taught me, or caught me when I stumbled. I hear the mountain's whisper, the river's song, the wolf's howl, the spirits' gentle guidance. And in their harmonious blend, I recognize what has always been there —a love that precedes and survives us all, a love into which we can surrender completely and find ourselves not diminished, but expanded beyond measure.

This journey continues—one step, one breath, one surrender at a time—into the luminous mystery that awaits, just beyond the next step, the next breath, the next letting go."

INVITATION TO PAUSE

- Where in your life right now might you need to take "one step at a time" rather than focusing on the distant summit? What becomes possible when you honor just the next step?
- Consider a challenge you're facing now. What if you approached it like navigating switchbacks in the dark—

focusing only on the next safe step rather than the overwhelming whole?

- Think of someone who caught you when you were falling—physically, emotionally, or spiritually. How did that experience of being held change your understanding of strength?
- What would it mean to embrace your life's "descent" with the same reverence you brought to its ascents?

SACRED INVITATION

"The door has always been within,
and the key has always been Love."

Every crack in your heart has been a doorway. Every ache a call. And that call has always been leading you home—not to a place, but to yourself. You are Love. You always have been. Not the fleeting kind that comes and goes. Not the kind that needs to be earned. But the very essence of Love itself.

If these pages found their way into your hands, I trust it wasn't by chance. There is a wisdom that guides us, even when—especially when —the path seems uncertain.

I come to you not as someone who has mastered surrender, but as a fellow traveler who has glimpsed what becomes possible when we yield to something greater than ourselves. The stories I've shared aren't offered as achievements, but as moments when love found its way through my resistance, my fear, my grasping for control.

What I've discovered in the quiet spaces between striving is this: You are already what you seek. The love you long for is not something to attain—it is what you are made of. The peace that feels so elusive isn't waiting somewhere else—it rests within you, patient as breath, steady as heartbeat.

THIS IS THE SACRED INVITATION

It is not a call to become more—but to become less. Not to become more spiritual, more enlightened, more anything. But to become less afraid, less guarded, less certain, less attached. To let what has always been true emerge through the opening of your surrendered heart.

I've spent decades learning this simple truth: surrender isn't passive resignation. It's active alignment with the love that moves the stars and whispers in the wind. It's the courage to stand in the fire of what is, rather than hide in the shadow of what might be.

When we step out of our own way—when we loosen our grip on how things should be—we enter a different kind of relationship with life. Not as managers trying to control outcomes, but as dancers moving in harmony with what wants to emerge.

Every morning, I ask myself: What will love choose today? How will love move through this situation, this conversation, this choice? Not as a concept, but as a living presence?

I invite you to try this. Not because it will make your life easier—it may not—but because it will make your life truer.

More spacious. More alive.

THE QUIETEST TEACHING

If we could strip away all spiritual traditions to their essence, what might remain? Perhaps just this:

You are not apart from what you seek.

You are not broken.

You are not lost.

The path home isn't complicated, though our minds often make it so. It's as simple and as challenging as this: return to the present moment, again and again. Feel your feet on the earth. Notice your breath. Let your attention rest in your heart.

In that simplicity, something profound happens. The noise of the world quiets. The voice of love grows clearer. Not as something outside you, but as the truest part of who you are.

I've found this teaching not just in moments of great beauty, but in times of deep loss. In the silence of meditation and the sweat of martial arts. In the touch of healing work and the tender vulnerability of relationships. The doorway appears in unexpected places, but it always opens to the same truth: love is your essence.

YOUR UNIQUE LIGHT

No teacher, no tradition, no book—including this one—can give you what you already have. They can only point to it, like a finger gesturing toward the moon.

Don't mistake the finger for the moon.

Your path will not look like mine or anyone else's. The divine does not repeat itself. You are an expression of love that has never existed before and will never exist again. Your way of embodying truth, your way of surrendering, your way of serving—these are uniquely yours.

Trust this. Honor it. Let it guide your walk.

In the wisdom traditions, teachings often come through the voice of those who have walked the path before us.

If a great teacher were to speak today, they might say:

"You were never apart from what you seek. The peace you long for is within you. The love you ache for is not missing—it is who you are. The light you pray for is already shining. You have only to turn inward and remember."

They might remind us that awakening is not about leaving the world behind—but loving it more deeply, more tenderly, more courageously.

"This world does not need more perfection. It needs more presence, more tenderness, more compassion, more loving kindness. More people willing to live as love, even when—especially when—it's hard."

And then they would grow quiet. And in that silence, you would feel it—the presence that has always been within: your essence, remembered.

In Aikido, we begin by imitating forms precisely. But mastery comes when those forms dissolve into spontaneous movement—when we no longer think about technique but simply respond with presence. This is true for the spiritual journey as well. We learn from traditions and teachers, but freedom comes when we allow our unique expression to emerge.

You are not here to become someone else's version of awakened. You are here to become fully yourself—radiantly, compassionately, imperfectly human.

The divine manifests uniquely through you. Your presence in this world—with your particular gifts, challenges, and perspectives—is a once-in-eternity phenomenon that carries its own sacred purpose.

You are not here to imitate.

You are here to illuminate.

Be that.

Fully.

Simple Practices

If you're wondering how to begin or deepen this journey of surrender, I offer these simple practices:

Pause and Feel: Several times each day, stop whatever you're doing. Take a few conscious breaths. Feel your body. Notice what's present without trying to change it. This tiny gap in the momentum of doing creates space for being.

Ask and Listen: Before responding to challenging situations, pause and silently ask: "What will love choose now?" Then wait. Listen not with your mind but with your heart. The answer may come as a feeling, an image, a sense of rightness.

Release the Small Self: When you notice yourself caught in worry, defensiveness, or control, place a hand on your heart and whisper: "I surrender this to love." Feel what shifts when you step out of your own way.

Practice Presence with Others: When someone speaks to you, give them your full attention. Listen without planning your response. See if you can feel their essence beyond their words. This is love in action.

Living as Prayer: Consider how you might live as prayer rather than someone who prays. Allow each moment to be an opportunity to practice presence—whether washing dishes with full attention to the sensation of water and the gleam of clean surfaces, or holding space for a friend's grief without rushing to solutions.

Let your presence itself become the offering. These aren't techniques to master but invitations to practice presence. Sometimes they will flow easily. Other times, they might feel impossible. All of it is part of the path. The path of surrender isn't something to perfect—it is an invitation, moment by moment, to surrender into love. It's not a destination—it's a continuous unfolding. All of it is the path.

A Moment of Silence

Take a breath now. Let these words fall away.
Feel the presence that remains when all concepts dissolve.
That presence is what you are.

Your Sacred Invitation

In your own words, what is love inviting you toward? What wants to emerge through your surrendered heart? What truth keeps appearing in your life, asking to be recognized?

Write your own Sacred Invitation—a letter from your heart to your life.

As you reflect on your own invitation, remember that this journey unfolds uniquely for each of us, yet always leads to the same truth.

A Gentle Closing

I offer these stories and reflections not as answers but as companionship on the journey. If even one word has awakened something within you—a remembering, a softening, a coming home to yourself—then sharing these pages has been worth it.

As you close this book, remember that the most profound spiritual practice isn't found in special circumstances but in how we meet ordinary moments. In how we wash dishes and greet strangers. In how we hold both joy and sorrow. In how we choose love when fear rises.

"It is like a finger pointing away to the moon. Don't concentrate on the finger or you will miss all that heavenly glory."

— BRUCE LEE

These words, these stories—they are only fingers pointing toward something far more vast, more luminous. The truth lives in your direct experience, in moments when you touch the sacred within the ordinary.

You don't need to search for it.

You only need to notice what has always been here.

The door has always been within,

and the key has always been Love.

In Love,

Tammy Lee Anderson

EPILOGUE

LOVE'S ECHO

"Before a mountain rises, the earth must give way. Strength is not what we carry—it's what rises after we fall."

I sit now in the quiet of an early morning, the kind of stillness that once cradled me as a child beneath a plum tree or steadied me on a kayak slicing through dawn's mirror. The journey of these stories—spanning a lifetime from that first fragile breath to this moment of reflection—has brought me here, to a place where surrender no longer feels like a lesson to learn, but a song I've always known. It's a melody woven through every crossing, every loss, every unexpected grace—a harmony humming beneath the surface of all things, waiting for us to listen.

Looking back, I see how each chapter built toward this truth: surrender isn't an end, but a beginning. It began in a hospital room where I floated in radiant peace, an infant unaware that love was calling me back to breath. It grew in the small closet where I hid from a world too loud, in the chapel where memory flooded through a priest's prayer, in the dojo where I learned to turn with force rather than against it. It deepened on rivers and roads, in monasteries and mountains, through the ache of losing my brother and the wonder of hearing him laugh beyond the veil.

And it blossomed fully in the stillness of mediumship, where I became a bridge—not the builder, but the crossing itself—carrying whispers of love from one world to another.

This path wasn't linear; it spiraled, doubling back on itself like a river finding its way home. The Air Force taught me to stand in my truth, honoring my inner voice even when facing pressure to conform, the mat showed me harmony in motion, and spirit revealed connection beyond form.

Each story—whether facing a wolf's challenge, healing without touch, or sketching a face guided by unseen hands—echoes the same refrain: what felt like struggle was often a doorway, and what seemed like loss was love reshaping itself. Even now, as I write, I feel the presence of those I've loved—Papa's steady chime, Cassie's gentle light, my brother's playful tease—reminding me that nothing is truly lost, only transformed.

What I've come to know is this: surrender is love's echo, a sound that reverberates through time and silence, binding us to each other and to the infinite. It's not passive; it's an active trust, a blending that opens us to what we cannot control but can embrace and harmonize with. In the Andean peaks, I carried soil from one sacred place to another, a gesture of connection; in Japan, I received a scroll tying my dojo to a lineage of peace. These acts mirror what this life has been—a bridge, a thread, a surrender into the luminous web that holds us all.

Perhaps you've heard this echo too—in a moment of letting go, in a connection that defies explanation, in the quiet after a storm. This book isn't my story alone; it's ours. It's an invitation to see your own crossings —your battles, your silences, your loves—as part of that same web. I once thought I was a warrior fighting to survive, then a seeker chasing meaning. But now I see I've been a co-creator all along, surrendering into love's vast embrace.

As I close this memoir, I light a candle, its flame dancing as it did in those locked-down days when those in spirit first communicated their messages of love. The wax transforms as it yields to heat, just as we transform when yielding to love. The light holds steady, illuminating what has always been true—the love that preceded my birth, that carries me now, that will outlast these words. It's not mine to keep, but to share—so I offer it to you: a whisper, a thread, a truth that surrender isn't the end of the story, but its eternal beginning. In that yielding, we find each other—and ourselves—whole, luminous, and forever one.

ABOUT THE AUTHOR

Tammy Lee Anderson, M.A., M.S., is a spiritual medium, distance healer, and intuitive guide whose extraordinary journey reveals the transformative power of surrender.

From early experiences as a competitive athlete and brief military service, Tammy discovered her true calling through more than a decade of monastic silence and a lifelong devotion to Aikido, earning a 5th-degree black belt—discovering that authentic strength lies not in force, but in flowing with life's currents.

With advanced degrees in Theology and Philosophy, Kinesiology and Exercise Physiology, and Marriage and Family Therapy, she weaves together science and spirit with uncommon grace. Her three near-death experiences became sacred thresholds—doorways to the unseen—that illuminate the heart of her spiritual practice and this memoir.

For over thirty years, Tammy has offered healing and guidance across five continents, witnessing again and again how body, mind, and soul speak as one. Her path has wound from Andean mountaintops to Japanese temples, from California sweat lodges to desert monasteries— each step deepening her understanding of surrender's quiet wisdom.

Today, she serves clients worldwide as a medium, healer, and compassionate witness—living proof that love transcends form and connection endures beyond death. Through her writing, teaching, and spiritual work, Tammy embodies a simple truth: when we release our grip and begin truly listening, surrender becomes our way home—to wholeness, to healing, and to Love.

⊕ **healingwellness.com**

****

A Heartfelt Request

If "*Into Love*" has resonated with you, please consider leaving your review on Amazon.

Reviews—however brief—helps other readers discover this book when they're searching for healing, hope, or understanding about love and loss.

Amazon's algorithm shows books to more people as reviews accumulate, meaning your words could be the reason someone else finds exactly what they need in their darkest hour. **Even a simple "This book helped me" with a star rating makes a difference.**

You can find the book by searching "*Into Love"* Tammy Lee Anderson" on Amazon.

Thank you for being part of this circle of healing and connection.

GLOSSARY

Aikido: A Japanese martial art developed by Morihei Ueshiba that focuses on blending with an attacker's energy rather than opposing it directly; literally translated as "the way of harmonizing energy."

Dojo: A training hall or practice space for martial arts; literally "place of the way" in Japanese. Traditionally considered a sacred space where students not only learn techniques but develop character and spiritual awareness.

Fascia: The connective tissue that wraps and connects muscles, bones, and organs throughout the body, forming a continuous three-dimensional web.

Fudoshin: A Japanese martial arts concept of the "immovable mind" or unshakable center that remains stable amid change and challenge.

Hakama: The traditional pleated skirt-like garment worn in Aikido by advanced practitioners, originally derived from samurai attire.

K1, K2, K4 : Olympic style racing kayaks: K1: single person kayak, K2: Two person kayak, K4: Four person kayak

Ki: The Japanese concept of life energy or vital force that flows through all living things and can be cultivated through practice.

Luminous Web: The interconnected network of energy and consciousness that links all beings and aspects of existence (a central metaphor throughout this memoir).

Medium/Mediumship: The practice of communicating with those who have passed into the non-physical realm, serving as a bridge between worlds.

Misogi: A Shinto purification ritual and martial arts concept; in Aikido, it refers to practices that purify the mind, body, and spirit. O-Sensei viewed the art itself as a form of misogi —training that cleanses practitioners of discord and disharmony.

Mushin: A Zen philosophy and martial arts concept of the state of "no-mind" where actions arise spontaneously without deliberate thought.

O-Sensei: Literally "Great Teacher," the honorific title given to Morihei Ueshiba (1883-1969), the founder of Aikido. His spiritual experiences led him to develop a martial art based on harmony rather than conflict, emphasizing that true victory comes through peace and reconciliation.

Pachamama: An Andean deity representing Mother Earth and fertility, central to indigenous spiritual practices encountered in Peru.

Piezoelectric: The property of certain crystals and biological materials (including fascia) to generate an electrical charge in response to mechanical pressure.

Randori: In martial arts Randori refers to free-style practice, multiple attackers at once, called the dance of chaos. The practice is to stay centered, like the center of a storm as you take your attackers down.

Rolf Structural Integration: A form of bodywork developed by Dr. Ida Rolf that aims to organize the body in relation to gravity through manipulation of the fascia.

Senshin: A Japanese martial arts concept of the "purified spirit" or enlightened attitude that represents the highest development of character.

Shoshin: A Japanese martial arts concept of the "beginner's mind" from Zen Buddhism—an attitude of openness and lack of preconceptions regardless of one's level of experience.

Shugyo: A Japanese concept of intensive training or severe ascetic practice undertaken to polish one's character and deepen spiritual understanding. In martial arts, it refers to dedicated practice that transcends mere technical development to become a path of personal transformation.

Surrender: As used in *Surrendering Into Love*, not giving up but consciously yielding to a greater flow, choosing to align with rather than resist life's currents.

Tenkan: An Aikido movement principle involving turning or pivoting to redirect energy, often used as a metaphor for changing perspective in life.

Ukemi: The art of receiving technique in Aikido; literally "receiving body," it involves learning to fall safely and respond appropriately to techniques.

Vipassana: A meditation technique focused on developing insight through mindful awareness of bodily sensations, thoughts, and feelings.

Vipassana Noble Silence: The practice of complete verbal and non-verbal silence during Vipassana meditation retreats to facilitate deeper awareness.

Zanshin: A Japanese martial arts concept of the state of relaxed awareness and continued connection after a technique is completed.

ALSO BY TAMMY LEE ANDERSON

The Ultimate Healer: Healing Meditation (audio)

To order : https://hemi-sync.com/product/the-ultimate-healer/

Printed in Dunstable, United Kingdom